FIELDS OF GOLD

Alex Jones

# FIELDS OF GOLD

OBERON BOOKS
LONDON

First published in 2005 by Oberon Books Ltd
521 Caledonian Road, London N7 9RH
Tel: +44 (0) 20 7607 3637 / Fax: +44 (0) 20 7607 3629
e-mail: info@oberonbooks.com
www.oberonbooks.com

A catalogue record for this book is available from the British Library.

ISBN: 978-1-84002-528-6

Cover design: Andrzej Klimowski

Visit www.oberonbooks.com to read more about all our books and to buy them. You will also find features, author interviews and news of any author events, and you can sign up for e-newsletters so that you're always first to hear about our new releases.

*for Jill Fraser,*
*my champion*

*I would like to thank
Laurie Sansom, Laura Harvey and Alan Ayckbourn
from the Stephen Joseph Theatre,
and Melvyn Sanders, friend and farmer.*

# Characters

BEN/BERNARD
mid forties

LILY
early seventies

MAGS
early forties

JULE/JULIE
twenty-one

JEM
seventeen

DAVE
mid twenties

The Handley family all speak with a Cumbrian accent;
Dave speaks with a London accent.

The action takes place in and around Handley Farm
in Cumbria, during the devastating foot and mouth
epidemic of 2001.

*Fields of Gold* was first performed at the Stephen Joseph Theatre, Scarborough, on 28 October 2004, with the following cast:

BEN, Colin MacLachlan

MAGS, Susan Twist

LILY, Judy Wilson

JULE, Claire Lams

JEM, Andrew Turner

DAVE, Andrew Brooke

*Director* Laurie Sansom

*Designer* Jessica Curtis

*Lighting Designer* Oliver Fenwick

*Sound Designer* Ben Vickers

# ACT ONE

## Scene 1

*The kitchen in the Handley's farmhouse. There is an Aga, a fireplace with a mantelpiece, a big wooden table with chairs around it, a sofa, and two doors, one of which leads to the stairs, the other to the hall and front door. Although the kitchen is cluttered with various farming implements, it is still cozy and clean. MAGS and BEN are sitting at the table eating their breakfast. BEN squirms in his chair.*

BEN: Sorry my fart smells.

MAGS: Everybody's farts smell.

BEN: Not like mine.

> (*Pause.*)

MAGS: You moved the cows yet?

BEN: Not yet.

MAGS: When yer movin' 'em then?

BEN: Ah doan't know, soon ah s'pose.

MAGS: They finished with yon pasture. You said they need movin'.

BEN: Ah know ah did.

> (*Pause.*)
> I farted again.
> (*Pause.*)
> 'S a ripe 'n' that.

MAGS: (*Sniffs.*) Shouldn't've had that curry last night.

BEN: 'S a balti, en't it? Bit strong on the old arse-ring.

MAGS: Spare the details, eh Ben? Anyway, doan't know what ye're doin' spendin' money on a take-away when we're so broke.

BEN: Bloody 'ell, gorra have a treat now an' again!

MAGS: Ah could've med a curry.

BEN: *You* mek a curry?!

MAGS: Some fancy vegetables an' yan of them Homepride Cook-in sauces.

BEN: En't the same.

MAGS: Yer got another bottle of whiskey, an' arl.

BEN: Doan't miss a trick, you.

MAGS: Gorra be careful; every penny counts.

BEN: Wha's life for?

MAGS: I'm jest sayin'...

BEN: What's life fer if yer can't 'ave a curry now an' then?

(*Long pause.*)

MAGS: Yer movin' the cows then?

BEN: Not reet at this moment, no.

MAGS: No, 'cause ye're too busy fartin'!

(*Pause.*)

You sin 'em this mornin'?

BEN: Nah, not yet.

MAGS Should tek a look.

BEN: We're safe enough out 'ere.

MAGS: Should still tek a look.

BEN: I will tek a bloody look if yer gie me a chance... *bleedin' 'ell!*

MAGS: En't no need ter swear all the time.

BEN: Aye...well.

MAGS: No need at arl.

BEN: Aye...alreet...sorry.

MAGS: Should think so. 'S bad enough hearin' it from Lily.

BEN: She can't 'elp it.

MAGS: Mebbe not, but it jest dun't sound reet – a woman of her age.

(*Pause.*)

So they're alreet, the cows?

BEN: Leave the frettin' ter me.

MAGS: I got a right t' know...

BEN: Aas the one who's responsible for farm.

MAGS: We're all responsible.

BEN: Yer doan't need ter worry.

MAGS: Aye, yer can say that...

(*BEN swigs his tea.*)

BEN: Oh, alreet if it'll shut you up ah'll go an' move 'em…! If the aliens en't had 'em.

MAGS: Well if we 'ave any more landin's we're ganna be in deep trouble.

BEN: We'll settle the feed bill end o' next month. It's all in hand.

MAGS: So yer say.

(*The door suddenly bursts open and LILY charges in. She has a tatty bunch of flowers in her hand.*)

LILY: *You bunch of bastards!!*

BEN: (*Shaken.*) For Christ sake!

LILY: You bunch of claggy bastards!

MAGS: Mornin' Lily, moderate yer language please.

LILY: 'S enough t' mek me bleedin' well cuss!

BEN: Calm down, Mam.

LILY: Doan't you tell me ter calm down. Who's the bloody parent 'ere? You do as ye're told, lad or ah'll gie thee such a clout, as big as you are.

BEN: Sit down.

LILY: (*Clouts him.*) Doan't you shout yer orders t' me, yer claggy twat!

MAGS Tha's a new 'n'; ah'm not even sure what it means.

BEN: That hurt.

LILY: Ah warned thee, din't I?

BEN: (*Sighs.*) So what is it now?

LILY: The bathroom.

BEN: Wha's wrong wi' bathroom?

LILY: How the bloody hell should ah know?

BEN: What thee talkin' about, Mam?

LILY: Yon bathroom, yer little tosser!

MAGS: (*Sighs.*)

BEN: Wha's wrong wi' it?

LILY: It's gone!

BEN: It's gone?

LILY: Yer know it's gone!

BEN: Where to?

LILY: How the bloody hell should ah know? You tell me.

BEN: Ah doan't know where it's gone.

LILY: How am ah s'posed t' have a shit if I can't find bathroom? How am ah ganna have a bath?

BEN: The bathroom en't gone. It's where it's allus bin.

LILY: Yer moved it!

BEN: How can ah move a bathroom?

LILY: Never mind how – *why?* Why did yer move it? You tryin' to torment me?

BEN: Ah can't move a bathroom during night. It's a major construction job.

LILY: Tha's what meks it so bloody galling!

MAGS: The bathroom's where it's allus bin, Lily.

BEN: Next ter Jem's room.

LILY: The bathroom's never bin next ter Jem's room.

BEN: Well where wuz it then?

LILY: You know where it wuz – across landing from my room!

BEN: Tha's our room.

LILY: Doan't you cum it wi' me, boy! Ye've moved it an' ye'd better tell me where.

MAGS: It's next ter Jem's room, Lily.

LILY: It had better be. (*Exiting.*) An' if yer move it again ah'm gonna brain you, yer bloody loony!

BEN: You off fer a bath, then?

LILY: If tha's alreet wi' you?

MAGS: Immersion's on, should be hot enough.

LILY: This place is like a madhouse! Movin' bloody bathrooms; never heard the like.

(*She exits, slamming the door behind her.*)

(*Off.*) *You mad bastard!*

(*Pause.*)

BEN: What a lovely start ter the day!

MAGS: Fairly routine, ah'd say.

BEN: I could strangle the daft cow sometimes.

MAGS: She's still yer Mam.

BEN: More's the pity.

LILY: (*Shouts off.*) *Bernard!*

BEN: Oh Christ, 'ere we go again!

(*LILY enters.*)

LILY: Oh here you are! Bin searching all ower.

BEN: Thought yer wor ganna 'ave a bath, Mam?

LILY: Aas in a minute. Wuz out this mornin'.

BEN: Oh aye, where'd yer go?

LILY: Top meadow.

BEN: What were yer doin' there, then?

(*Produces the bunch of wild flowers now behind her back.*)

LILY: Picked some flowers. For Maggie, really.

MAGS: (*Takes them.*) Oh Lily, they're lovely!

LILY: Pretty 'n's, en't they?

MAGS: They're lovely!

LILY: Well you know – en't much I can do round 'ere. I know ah'm a bit of a pain, but ah want yer ter know how much I appreciate yer lettin' me cum back.

BEN: It's as much your farm as ours.

LILY: Ah know that, but all the same…

MAGS: (*Kisses her.*) Ye're welcome 'ere, Lily, doan't worry none…ah'll get a vase for these.

LILY: En't no shit on 'em.

MAGS: No.

LILY: 'Cause there's shit all ower them fields.

BEN: Allus is.

LILY: Well you oughta do summat about it, lad. It's a bloody disgrace! Need a kick up the arse!

BEN: 'S the cows, en't it?

LILY: No need blamin' the cows, lad! Your old Da', wouldn' let 'em get away wi' that. You tidy it up.

BEN: Alreet, Mam.

LILY: Shit all ower the fields…can smell it in 'ere an' arl.

BEN: Aye well, doan't yer worry none. Ah'll sort it out.

LILY: See yer do… Well, ah'll gan an' 'ave me bath, then. Doan't go movin' it again, will yer? (*Exiting.*) Bloody stupid thing ter do, that.

(*She meets JEM, who is entering the room as she leaves.*)

JEM: Mornin' Nan!

LILY: Mornin' young 'n'. You 'elp yer Da' tidy that field up.

JEM: Aye, alreet.

> (*LILY has gone. JEM sits at the table.*)

> There's bin another landin'.

MAGS: Oh not another!

JEM: Aye, can see it from my room.

BEN: Wha's the damage?

JEM: Looks like a big craft. Not the mother ship, like; probably a scout ship.

BEN: If I get hold of 'em, the bloody swines!

MAGS: *All that corn!*

JEM: They've got their eyes on this place, alreet.

BEN: 'S the bloody army, ah reckon.

MAGS: No Ben, 's just a bunch o' kids messin' about.

JEM: No – 's the aliens.

MAGS: 'S just a bunch of kids larkin' about.

BEN: Well if I catch 'em, ah'll put another hole up their arse!

MAGS: Doan't get goin' out wi' that gun again.

JEM: Guns are no use 'gainst their technology.

BEN: Ruinin' a poor man's livelihood! Scarin' the stock an' arl.

MAGS: (*With teapot.*) Want some tea?

JEM: Thanks.

BEN: Ohh…*bloody corn!*

MAGS: Mebbe it en't much.

JEM: It is – great big circle wi' three little 'n's round it. *Should see it!*

BEN: 'S the army!

MAGS: It en't the army.

BEN: Bloody army wallahs playin' their silly games again. Think they own the place they do. Can't step ower the top field wi'out some soddin' tin 'ead blowin' a whistle, goin' doo-bloody-lalley!

MAGS: It's the range. It's fer your own safety.

BEN: Ye're beginnin' t' sound like 'em!

JEM: I bin ower there lots o' times.

MAGS: Well you stay away – 's dangerous.

JEM: Tha's where the aliens are.

BEN: Why doan't they bomb the little green gits, then? Stop 'em mashin' my corn, do summat bloody useful, 'stead o' blowin' the countryside ter pieces?

MAGS: They gorra practice somewhere. 'Sides most o' the shells land in sea.

BEN: *Bloody army!*

MAGS: Can't blame the army fer everythin'.

BEN: Why not?

MAGS: Obsessed, you are.

JEM: Could be their planet's dyin'…tha's what I think, anyroad. (*JULE enters.*)

JULE: Nan said yer moved the bathroom.

BEN: Aye, but I put it back.

JULE: (*Sniffs.*) You bin eatin' them curries again?

BEN: 'S a balti, 'n' it?

JULE: Dun't think they agree wi' yer. (*Sits at the table.*) Sin the news yet this mornin'?

BEN: Ah doan't wanna see anymore pictures of cattle bein' burned thank you very much; some BBC bloke in a suit slaggin' off farmers!

JEM: Well it *were* farmers' fault, weren' it?

BEN: *Pig farmer.*

JEM: Still a farmer.

MAGS: Can we all settle down an' 'ave our breakfast, please?

BEN: There's another crop circle.

JULE: Oh bloody 'ell! Big 'n'?

JEM: Reckon it wor a scout ship.

JULE: Is that big?

JEM: Not as big as the mother ship, but still pretty big.

MAGS: 'S them kids from the estate, ah reckon.

BEN: 'S the army.

JULE: It en't the army.

MAGS: Ah said that.

BEN: Bunch o' camouflaged hooligans, probably think it's a
    great joke!
    (*There is a distant thud as bombing starts on the range.*)
    *Bloody 'ell! What time is it?!*

MAGS: Eight o' clock, gone.

BEN: *Eight o' bloody clock* an' they're bombin' already!

JEM: Pity they dun't drop a bomb on this place.

MAGS: Doan't you speak about yer 'ome like tha'!

JULE: Gerrin' worse, he is.

JEM: *Up yours!*

JULE: Goin' on about aliens all the time. You wanna get out a bit.

JEM: You wanna stay in a bit.

JULE: Least I got a life.

JEM: Call that a life, jiggin' yer tits at bloody clubs all night?

MAGS: (*Warning.*) 'Ey -

JULE: Ye're just jealous!

JEM: Jealous o' you?!

JULE: (*Smiles.*) I reckon you wanna *be* me.

JEM: In yer dreams!

MAGS: Pack it in you pair!

JEM: I got a life; ganna mek contact soon.

JULE: *Sad git!*

JEM: They bin 'ere again, en't they?

JULE: Ah think we'd've noticed a bloody great spaceship
    landin' on corn.

JEM: Not if they wor usin' a cloakin' device.

BEN: *Shut up the pair of yer!* Crikey, 's like a bloody soap opera
    in 'ere some mornings.

MAGS: Aye, well we know where they get it from, dun't we?

BEN: Wha's that supposed ter mean?

MAGS: Hardly Mr Sunshine, lately, are yer?

BEN: Excuse me, but who's doin' all the arguing 'ere?

MAGS: Should set an example.

BEN: I en't done 'owt!

MAGS: Well mebbe yer should – them cows fer a start off.

BEN: Reet, ah'll go an' move 'em then. Mind if ah finish me tea first… *crikey.* (*To JEM.*) 'N' you – get yer lazy arse off ter school!

JEM: I en't gannin'.

BEN: Yer bloody are!

JEM: Ah'm not.

MAGS: Ye've got ter go ter school, Jem. Everybody needs qualifications these days. Look at yer sister – she's got a first class diploma now.

JEM: *In agriculture?!*

MAGS: 'Ey, yer sister's done very well ter get that diploma.

JEM: Doan't need a diploma ter milk a cow.

JULE: What d'*you* know about farmin', anyroad?

JEM: Enough.

JULE: Yer can't even hold a shovel.

MAGS: Leave him alone, Jule.

BEN: She's reet. Wouldn't hurt him ter get stuck in now an' then. When ah was his age I was ploughin' an drillin', ah was.

JEM: Get the violins out.

MAGS: Y'can stop it, all on yer. I en't havin' this ower breakfast.

BEN: Stroke o' dawn ah wuz up.

JULE: So what? Ah've bin up nearly two hours already.

JEM: Wha's this? A misery competition?

BEN: Doan't know what hard work is.

MAGS: Now I said tha's enough!

BEN: 'Bout time he pulled his weight.

JULE: All he pulls is his plonker.

JEM: Aye, well you'd know ah s'pose, bein' an expert on plonkers.

JULE: Like ah said – jealous, yer sad little virgin.

MAGS: I en't havin' that kind o' talk in my house! *Now stop it.*

BEN: Up an' down' fields: *rain, snow, hail…*

JULE: Aas in the fields 'afore you. Aas allus out there first.

BEN: Ah keep me eye on this farm. Ah'm alluss doin' summat: accounts, plannin'…

JULE: *Plannin'?* You en't changed 'owt fer years.

17

BEN: Ah've told yer a thousand times – aas not changin' farm ter suit your wacky ideas! Spent two bloody years at college an' thinks yer knows it arl!

JEM: I'm giein' up sixth form.

BEN: No ye're bloody not.

JEM: Ah'm seventeen, ah can please meself.

BEN: Not in my 'ouse yer can't. Ye're goin'.

JEM: So *mek me!*

BEN: Ye're goin' t' school!

JEM: I en't!

JULE: We *should* be goin' organic.

BEN: What?!

MAGS: Not now, Jule.

JULE: Stuck in a rut, you are.

(*BEN is about to come back at them when there are suddenly more explosions outside. BEN grabs his gun.*)

BEN: *Eight o'clock, eight o' bloody clock!* Listen to 'em – blowin' the countryside ter pieces!

MAGS: Where yer gannin' wi' that gun?

BEN: Ah'm ganna fire a few off. Let 'em know ah can mek a noise an' arl.

(*BEN begins to exit.*)

MAGS: Ben…! You are not ter stir things up out there…

(*But he has gone.*)

Obsessed, he is. Ah'd better gan an' keep me eye on him.

(*To JEM.*) Get theeself ter school, you!

(*MAGS exits.*)

(*Calling off.*) Now, jest calm down, Ben…!

(*Pause.*)

JEM: I en't goin'.

(*JULE shakes her head in disgust. Music. Lights fade to blackout.*)

# Scene 2

*The cornfield. Approaching dusk, the same day. JEM is sitting in the corn by the boundary fence, looking at the sky with binoculars. JULE approaches with a carrier bag.*

JULE: Lookin' fer aliens?

JEM: Yeah.

JULE: Wanna fag? (*Tosses baccy and rizlas.*).

JEM: Aw, thanks Jule!

JULE: Beer?

JEM: Great.

    (*Takes four-pack from carrier, tears one off and hands it to JEM. He takes a small packet from his pocket.*)

    Got some blow. Ah'll roll us one up.

JULE: *Nice one!*

JEM: Dad calmed down?

JULE: Not really.

JEM: What is it now?

JULE: Had a phone call; can't move cows.

JEM: But we need ter move 'em.

JULE: There's bin a case confirmed at a farm near Eskdale.

JEM: Tha's miles away!

JULE: Well MAFF says we can't move 'em.

JEM: Eskdale's's miles away. Our herd's clear.

JULE: 'S MAFF, en't it? En't tekin' no chances.

JEM: Soddin' 'ell! 'S like the Gestapo.

JULE: Well he's gerrin' the disinfectant out, anyroad.

JEM: Aw shit!

JULE: Bales o' straw down by gate. Yer could gie us a hand later.

JEM: We gorra disinfect ourselves everytime we cum an' go?

JULE: Looks that way.

JEM: Bloody rigmarole. Next thing they'll 'ave us walkin' around ringin' a bell shoutin' *'unclean'*.

JULE: 'S bin on the cards for years, this.

JEM: Oh God, doan't start on about arl that organic stuff again; 's borin'.

JULE: *You're* borin'.

(*JEM has finished rolling the joint. He lights up, takes a drag and sighs. He passes it over to JULE.*)

JEM: 'Ere, get yer laughin' gear round that –

JULE: (*Tokes.*) *Mm, nice!*

(*Pause.*)

Yer mean it, 'bout not goin' ter school?

JEM: Aye.

JULE: Dad's furious.

JEM: Dun't care.

JULE: Mam's worried ter death.

JEM: 'Ten't my fault.

JULE: *Why?*

JEM: Just dun't like it, tha's arl.

JULE: *Tha's arl?*

JEM: Tha's arl.

JULE: So what yer ganna do?

JEM: Dunno…summat.

JULE: *Waster!*

JEM: S'pose so.

(*Pause.*)

JULE: You bin in my underwear drawer again?

JEM: Yer what?

JULE: You bin messin' about wi' my underwear?

JEM: No! I en't touched yer bloody underwear.

JULE: 'Cause yer like ter wear my panties, dun't yer?

JEM: What?!! Where'd yer get that idea from?

JULE: They go missin' fer a couple o' days an' turn up again all crumpled.

JEM: Ah doan't know what ye're talkin' about.

JULE: Anyway ah'm 'avin' a bit of a clear out. Yer can 'ave 'em if yer like.

JEM: Ah doan't want yer panties!

JULE: Please yerself.

(*Pause.*)

JEM: Ah'll tek 'em to Oxfam though, if yer like.

JULE: Ah'll leave 'em outside me door in a plastic bag.

JEM: Okay…I'm goin' ter town; may as well drop 'em in.

JULE: So yer wun't need ter rifle my drawers anymore, will yer?

JEM: No…I mean *no, I never!*

JULE: Whatever.

(*Pause.*)

JEM: I wouldn' do 'owt like that. 'S not normal, is it?

JULE: No.

JEM: No, din't think it wuz.

JULE: But if yer enjoys it, wha's the problem?

JEM: Ah doan't enjoy it… I mean if I *did* I wouldn't, but ah don't…so I *don't*.

JULE: Whatever… (*Takes a drag at the joint.*) 'S good blow.

JEM: Got it from Mel.

JULE: You ever really sin an alien?

JEM: Oh I sin 'em alreet! Hear 'em an' arl sometime.

JULE: Well yer wanna tell 'em ter leave our corn alone. Lost a lot this time.

JEM: Ganna mek contact soon.

JULE: Barmy git.

JEM: You see.

(*Pause as they both drink and smoke.*)

(*Smiles.*) 'S nice this, en't it?

JULE: (*Nods.*)

(*A soldier suddenly stands up in the long grass at the other side of the boundary fence. He points a gun at them.*)

DAVE: Don't move!

(*Pause.*)

Don't move a muscle – this is a warning!

(*Pause.*)

What are you doin' so close to Ministry of Defence property?

JULE: Bugger you an' the army! This is our property this side o' fence.

DAVE: Really? What you doin' with those binoculars? You been spyin' on our activities?

JEM: Aye. What yer gun' ter do about it, yer khaki git?

DAVE: I don't have to take mouth from civilians. Put your hands up; I'm takin' you in.

JEM: Go an' 'ave a wank.

DAVE: Who d'you think you're talkin' to, *farmer boy?*

JEM: You – *army twat!*

DAVE: I'm not accustomed to insults.

JEM: Stick around a bit then.

DAVE: Know what I'm gonna do?

JULE: Surprise us.

DAVE: I'm gonna shoot yer…both.

JEM: Yer wouldn't dare.

DAVE: Wouldn't I?

JULE: Police'd have you soon as they found our bodies.

DAVE: (*Smiles.*) Who says they'll find your bodies? The army's got ways of disposing of embarrassing information. People disappear all the time.

JULE: Yer mean it, doan't yer? Ye're really ganna kill us.

DAVE: Yeah.

(*He lifts the gun to his shoulder and takes aim.*)

JULE: Nowt we can do ter change yer mind?

DAVE: No.

JEM: Would a can o' beer help?

(*Pause.*)

DAVE: Oh, all right then.

(*DAVE steps over the fence into the meadow, high-fives with JEM.*)

JEM: How goes it, Dave?

DAVE: Same as usual. (*Kisses JULE.*) Alright sweetheart?

JULE: Alreet darlin'.

DAVE: Giz a drag –

(*Takes a long drag at the joint.*)

Mm, that's better! (*Sighs.*) *What a day!*

JEM: You lot started early enough. Dad went doo-lalley; wuz on the range wi' his gun, firin' all around him.

DAVE: (*Cracking open a can.*) He wants to be careful.

JULE: Under pressure, ah reckon. What wi' disease gerrin' closer an' arl.

JEM: Woan't reach 'ere.

JULE: Could do, 's possible.

JEM: *Shit!*

JULE: Why're you suddenly so concerned anyhow? Ye're never ganna be a farmer.

JEM: Mebbe not, but it's still me home.

DAVE: Join the army; make a man of yer.

JULE: Doubt it.

JEM: (*Horrified she might spill the beans.*) *Jule!*

DAVE: I'm serious. I've had a great time; been all over the world: Germany, Belize, America. Give it a go –

JEM: Doan't think it's me, really.

JULE: Tha's a relief for the armed forces.

JEM: Leave off, Jule.

DAVE: Dunno what I'll do once me time's up. A lot of 'em end up in the Met.

JEM: Swap one uniform for another; meks sense.

DAVE: I'd have you in a cell straight away: *smoking illegal substances.*

(*Tokes.*) Your Dad should try some of this; might calm him down a bit. I'll pop round with an ounce of bush.

JEM: (*Laughs.*) *Like yeah!* He'd blow yer arse away.

JULE: Best stay away from the silly bastard at the moment. See yer in town t'night, eh?

DAVE: 'Bout time I called round, though. Said hello an' all that.

JULE: This en't the right time, believe me.

DAVE: Should introduce myself. I mean, pretty soon I'm gonna get me next posting.

JEM: She wun't go wi' yer.

DAVE: 'S up to her, Jem.

JEM: She's a farmer; she wun't live anywhere else.

DAVE: Could be posted any moment.

JEM: She wun't leave the farm, will yer Jule?

JULE: I like farmin'

DAVE: An' I...

JEM: ...*like killin'.*

DAVE: I've never killed anybody.

JEM: 'S yer job though, en't it?

DAVE: You lot kill all the time.

JEM: *Beasts,* yer.

DAVE: Still killin'.

JEM: *Animals.*

DAVE: Bunch of murderin' bastards, farmers.

JEM: Gorra keep the army in bacon butties, en't we?

JULE: Ah'm glad you en't killed anybody, Dave.

DAVE: Ditto darlin', ditto.

(*They kiss, briefly. JEM takes up his binoculars.*)

JEM: *I sin one!*

JULE: Bollocks!

JEM: Ah did – I sin one!

JULE: Where?

JEM: Streak o' light at the horizon.

DAVE: Probably a jet.

JEM: No it weren't. They're cummin', they're cummin'!

JULE: (*Indicating joint.*) You wanna leave off that stuff.

JEM: Yer missed it! It wor plain...bloody 'ell, yer missed it.

DAVE: Be a jet.

JEM: Not at that speed.

DAVE: Could be a comet, I s'pose.

JEM: *Green?*

DAVE: It was green?

JEM: 'S their fusion reactors – anti-gravity device, gives off
     rays, like.

JULE: Wish they'd beam you up.

DAVE: We'd know if there was anythin' out there, Jem. We've
     got radar all over the ranges.

JEM: Come off it, Dave. Wi' respect, mate; ye're just a bloody
     foot-soldier, lowest o' the low; they en't ganna tell you 'owt.

(*DAVE jumps on JEM and they wrestle on the ground.
     They all laugh, especially JEM.*)

DAVE: You cheeky little sod! Think you can talk to Her
   Majesty's finest like that?!
JULE: Go on, Dave – slit his scrawny little throat!
   (*DAVE quickly overpowers JEM and sits on him, pinning his
   hands to the ground.*)
JEM: Yeah? You an' whose army? (*Laughs.*) I shouldna' said
   that – you 'ave got an army, en't yer?
   (*They are all laughing.*)
DAVE: Yeah – take me to your leader!
   (*They all laugh again. LILY suddenly kneels up in the corn
   behind them. She has been watching them, concealed, and looks
   well angry. JULE senses someone watching, but when she turns
   to look, LILY has dived back into the corn.*)
JULE: Hey, shut up a minute!
DAVE: Wha's up?
JULE: Thought I 'eard summat.
   (*DAVE climbs off JEM. JEM remains on his back, smiling.*)
DAVE: It's bloody E-T!
JULE: Tell Dad an' he'll be out wi' his gun.
DAVE: You don't need yer Dad. I'll protect yer!
   (*They kiss. JEM watches. They clock on he's looking.*)
JULE: What you lookin' at?
JEM: Carry on – I en't gunna bother yer.
JULE: You are *not* gunna watch us messin' about!
JEM: I weren't ganna watch… Ah'm ganna look fer crafts.
DAVE: Go on, Jem – give us an hour, eh?
   (*JEM reluctantly stands up.*)
JULE: Here – (*Throws him a can.*) have another can.
JEM: Thanks.
   (*He's about to walk off, when he notices MAGS approaching.*)
   Mam's cummin'!
   (*JULE stubs the joint.*)
JULE: Dave –
DAVE: What?
JULE: Could yer…?
DAVE: What?

JULE: I en't told anyone yet, an' yer shouldn't be on land, really.

DAVE: Oh, come on Jule…

JULE: Jest this once, till ah've told 'em, like.

DAVE: You're a hard woman.

(*They kiss.*)

JULE: Talkin' about hard.

JEM: She's cummin'.

DAVE: I'll sort you out later.

(*DAVE dives into the corn.*)

MAGS: (*Approaching.*) You sin yer Nan?

JULE: No. How long's she bin missin'?

MAGS: Hours. Ah doan't know where she gets to.
(*Exasperated.*) Oh…silly woman! (*Sniffs.*) I can smell smoke.
You bin smokin'?

JEM: No.

MAGS: Bet you 'ave; bet yer smoke an' arl. Ye're goin' ter school t'morra'.

JEM: I en't.

MAGS: You blinkin' well are.

JEM: I bloody en't.

MAGS: Ye're ganna need yer qualifications, Jem.

JULE: Dad still in a mood?

MAGS: Jest sulkin' now, way he does.

JULE: (*Laughs.*) Buy him a curry, that'll cheer him up.

MAGS: No thanks; smell about the place…! Where has she got to? (*Shouts.*) Lily…! Ganna 'ave ter call the police again.
I hope she en't wandered off the farm.

JEM: Searched all the barns?

MAGS: 'Course we 'ave. An' the 'ouse top ter bottom. Yer Dad said ter leave it, she'll turn up.

JULE: Ah'm sure she will; does normally.

MAGS: Ah'm worried. She's bin much worse lately: proper agitated an' wound up, *'n' all that swearin'!* Ah divn't know she knew such words.

JULE: Everybody swears on farms.

MAGS: Help us search, will yer?

JULE: Aye…aye in a minute.

JEM: Cum on Mam, let's check the lane. She could be in the old chicken shed again.

MAGS: Hadn't thought o' that.

JEM: See yer when ah see yer.

JULE: Not if I see you first.

(*JEM and MAGS exit.*)

Coast's clear.

(*DAVE emerges from the corn and dives on JULE.*)

DAVE: *Come 'ere you sexy little bitch, you!*

JULE: Ooh…no, what you ganna do ter me, soldier boy?

(*They get stuck in.*)

Oh Dave…! *Oh God!*

DAVE: God an' all his angels, sweetheart!

(*LILY suddenly stands up in the corn, she looks down at them. She has a hefty branch of a tree in her hands.*)

LILY: You claggy bastard!

(*DAVE sits up, surprised.*)

DAVE: What?

(*LILY whacks him across his head with the branch and he falls to the ground. She begins to lay into him.*)

LILY: You bloody claggy army bastard!

(*JULE pulls her off him. They fall to the ground.*)

JULE: No Nan, no! What are yer doin'?!

LILY: The claggy army bastard!

(*She sits down and JULE goes to DAVE.*)

JULE: Dave…? Dave…?

(*He doesn't stir.*)

My God no, he's dead! (*Crying.*) *Ye've killed him! Ye've killed him, Nan!*

(*Music. Lights fade to blackout.*)

27

# Scene 3

*The house. The next morning. BEN is sitting at the table with the telephone.*

BEN: Hello… Ben Handley here… (*Laughs.*) Handley Farm, tha's reet. How are yer…? Good, aye grand…! Well I heard yer wuz lookin' fer a baler… About three years old, good nick…surplus ter requirements, like… Yeah…? Well ah divn't know – make me an offer, like… *How much…?* Oh cum on, Mr Davies, it's three years old…! Well ah wuz thinkin' more in the line of… No, no, let me think about it…er, we've got a rotavator too, 's a…reet jest the baler…aye…
(*MAGS enters with a bucket of potatoes.*)
Well…ah'll…look, ah'll get back ter yer. (*Rings off.*)

MAGS: Who's that?

BEN: Ah…jest, yer know another rep tryin' ter flog us summat.

MAGS: Aye?

BEN: Aye…get sick on it.

MAGS: Aye, they can get reet pushy. What wuz it?

BEN: What?

MAGS: What wuz it they wor tryin' ter sell us?

BEN: Ah, yer know…seed, fertiliser.
(*Pause.*)

MAGS: Ben…we gorra talk.

BEN: Oh…aye?

MAGS: I think it's time we faced up ter things.

BEN: Things are fine, pet… I admit, well yer know there's allus summat outstandin', but tha's farmin' these days – same wi' everybody.

MAGS: Ah'm not talkin' about farm, ah'm talkin' about Lily.

BEN: Me Mam, what about her?

MAGS: Look, this en't easy…

BEN: What en't easy?

MAGS: Well she's gerrin' worse, yer know she is; allus goin' missin', gerrin' confused an' ter top it arl – this business in cornfield.

BEN: She's happy 'ere, Mags.

MAGS: Is she? Ah'm not sure.

BEN: 'Mongst her own.

MAGS: Well…*ah'm* findin' it difficult. 'S like ah'm a full-time carer, an' ah've got enough ter do about place as it is.

BEN: She's me Mam.

MAGS: Ah know that, love…

BEN: End o' discussion.

MAGS: She's on'y ganna get worse, Ben.

BEN: End of discussion, Mags.

(*Pause.*)

MAGS: Aye…well alreet. Next thing we gorra talk about though is cows. Ah've bin thinkin' about it; we need ter tek precautions.

BEN: I have, yer know I have; put them carpet off-cuts cross lane an' arl, soaked 'em in disinfectant.

MAGS: Need ter do more than that. It's startin' ter get a real grip round 'ere.

BEN: Well…what more can I do?

(*LILY enters.*)

LILY: Got any All Brown, Mags?

MAGS: All Brown? Wha's that?

LILY: All Brown, ter mek yer shit; ah'm fair bunged up, I am.

MAGS: All *Bran*, Lily.

LILY: (*Slightly annoyed.*) Tha's what ah said – *All Brown!* Helps yer ter…

MAGS: (*Sighs.*) Ah know what it does. Sit yerself down, Lily. (*MAGS gets cereal, bowl, milk, etc. and sets it before LILY. She has to put cereal and milk in for her.*)

BEN: An' how's me Mam this mornin'?

MAGS: Bunged up! Are yer deaf as well as stupid? Ah need a good clear-out.

(*JEM enters.*)

JEM: Any chance o' some toast?

MAGS: Two slices?

JEM: Aye.

BEN: He should be at school. You had a word wi' him?

MAGS: Ah can't mek him go, can I?

BEN: *Lazy sod!* Get off ter school!

JEM: No.

BEN: You should obey me – ah'm yer father.

JEM: I'm en't gannin' anymore.

BEN: Who's in charge in this house?

LILY: Will yer stop pickin' on yon lad!

BEN: He's gorra go ter school, Mam.

LILY: You think ye're in charge, doan't yer?

BEN: Well… I…

LILY: Know who's in charge?

BEN: Well…

LILY: Answer me when I talk ter thee!

BEN: Ah…ah divn't know, Mam.

LILY: Yer Dad, that's who. It's his farm an' then yourn an' then Jem's. So shurrup!

JEM: Ah divn't want it.

LILY: 'Course yer want it.

JEM: It's Jule who wants it.

BEN: Dad's dead, Mam. Ah keep tellin' yer.

MAGS: Ben, will yer please be a bit more sensitive.

LILY: What a thing ter say! What a thing ter say about yer own father!

BEN: Well he's hardly about ter walk through door, is he? He's bin pushin' up daisies fer past four year.

MAGS: Insensitive, you are.

LILY: What a thing ter say!

BEN: (*Giving up.*) Oh giz a cup o' tea –

MAGS: 'S in the pot.

BEN: (*Ironic.*) Thanks a lot!

MAGS: *Who's in charge?* We all share this place as far as ah can see.

(*JULE enters.*)

JULE: Some tea, Mam?

*(MAGS rises and gets a mug for her.)*

MAGS: Sit yerself down, love. Ah'll pour yer one.

BEN: Marvellous! Pour *her* a bloody cup!

JULE: What?

MAGS: Oh ignore him.

LILY: You sin yer grandad this mornin', Julie?

JULE: He's dead.

LILY: Oh.

*(BEN looks for a reaction.)*

MAGS: Finished milkin' now?

JULE: Aye an' ah took some feed over t' meadow.

BEN: How's it lookin'?

JULE: 'S gerrin' bad. Grass is all but gone. When can we move 'em?

BEN: Ah dunno, when they says we can.

JULE: It'll be a quagmire if it rains.

LILY: Farm's yours then, Bernard.

BEN: What?

LILY: After aas gone. Farm's yours if yer Dad's dead. He *is* dead, en't he?

JEM: Definitely, Nan.

LILY: Wish people'd tell me these things.

BEN: 'S bin a while now, Mam.

LILY: So why keep me in dark? I can't mek you out, lad. Ye're an odd 'n' an' no mistakin'. What a thing ter do! You shoulda' told me. Things like that are important.

BEN: *(Sighs.)* *Ah've got a headache.*

MAGS: Not surprised the way yer put it away last night.

LILY: *Ah'm* constipated.

JEM: *(Laughs.)* Need a good shit, eh Nan?

MAGS: Alreet Jem, no need fer you ter join in.

LILY: Ah need a good shit…*if ah could find bathroom!*

*(Glares at BEN.)*

BEN: Ah could do wi' a drink now.

MAGS: Reet, now we're all together we need ter discuss farm.

JEM: Well – 's a load o' fields wi' animals an' crops in it.

JULE: *Funny!*

MAGS: Cum on everybody, ah'm bein' serious. Disease is gerrin' closer day by day. There's bin a case confirmed twenty miles away; we doan't wanna lose cows.

JULE: No way they're cullin' my herd!

MAGS: Which is why I reckon we should seal off the farm.

JEM: *Oh no!*

JULE: I en't stayin' in.

MAGS: 'S the thing ter do. No comin' an' goin'; nobody callin' round.

BEN: What about me curries?

MAGS: I think that's the last thing we need ter worry about.

JULE: *'What about yer curries?'* What about me life?!

JEM: Ah've gorra be able ter get out, Mam.

JULE: When d'you go out, anyroad?

JEM: Ah go out.

JULE: Where?

JEM: Me Sat'day job.

JULE: What a fulfillin' life yer lead.

JEM: Ah know what ye're worried about.

JULE: Careful what yer say, little boy.

JEM: Gerrin' yer end away.

MAGS: Yer know I doan't like that smutty kind of talk in 'ouse. *Cut it out now!*

LILY: *Army bastard!*

MAGS: Look – ye've set yer Nan off now. Yer shouldn't use words like that, Lily.

BEN: Right though, en't she?

JULE: Yer what?

BEN: Ganna get yerself a reet reputation, gannin' wi' the army.

JEM: Not the *whole* army.

JULE: Ah'm warnin' you –

JEM: Ah wor stickin' up for yer then, actually.

JULE: Divn't bother.

JEM: He's a nice bloke, Dave. I like him.

BEN: *Nice bloke?* He's a bloody soldier!

MAGS: Aw, he did seem nice, though. He din't make a fuss about Lily, either.

LILY: Who din't?

JEM: *Dave,* Nan – you remember in corn.

LILY: What thee talkin' about?

JEM: Had ter go to hospital; had concussion.

LILY: He wor rapin' Julie.

MAGS: He weren't rapin' her, Lily.

BEN: Well if he weren't rapin' her, she should be ashamed of herself.

MAGS: *What?!*

BEN: Lettin' him do…dirty stuff to her…*in the open air, an arl!*

LILY: Ah welt 'im one, ah did. Ah cracked his head open. (*Laughs.*).

MAGS: Yer shouldna' done it, Lily.

BEN: Well if we do seal 'place off, yer wun't be seein' *him* fer a while anyroad.

JULE: *Great!*

MAGS: We gorra do summat, Jule. Think o' the implications.

JULE: Aye, ye're reet, Mam. We need ter stick tergether ter beat this one.

JEM: Ah'll get plenn'y o' cans in; we'll be okay.

BEN: Ye're too young ter drink anyroad.

JEM: Just follerin' 'family tradition, Dad.

BEN: Ah'll gie thee such a clout one o' these days, yer cheeky sod!

JEM: (*Grins.*) Can't hit kids; 's illegal now.

LILY: Yer should call social services, Maggie; report him fer that; 's child abuse, that is.

BEN: Ah din't mean 'owt. 'S an expression, tha's arl.

LILY: Has he done 'owt sexual to yer, Jem?

BEN: *Ah beg yer bloody pardon?!*

LILY: 'Cause you 'ear about it, doan't yer? Ah mean it 'appens.

BEN: Mam, how can yer say such a thing? How could you think such a thing o' me? Aas yer son – aas Bernard, yer son.

LILY: Yer shouldn't threaten yer family wi' violence.

BEN: Christ, *you* caved Jule's boyfriend's 'ead in wi' half a
    soddin' tree!

LILY: Shoulda' sin what he wor doin' to her in' corn
    – *disgustin'!*

MAGS: They're a couple, Lily. Dave's her boyfriend.

LILY: (*Points at BEN.*) 'N' yer should report him ter social
    services. Yer know what thee wants, doan't yer?

BEN: Surprise me.

LILY: A psychiatrist.

BEN: Thanks.

LILY: A psychiatrist an' some o' them tablets that mek yer…
    (*Can't find the word.*)

BEN: Die?

LILY: (*Finds it.*) *Calm down.*

MAGS: Thank you, Lily tha's enough advice fer now. Le's
    start gerrin' stuff sorted. Ah'll start ringin' round; tell
    everyone ter stay away from farm.

JULE: Aye, we'll beat it: nobody's ganna kill my herd. Ah'll
    get some notices med up ter warn people away.

JEM: Ah'll help paint 'em, Jule. Aas good at art!

JULE: Ah'll be in old barn then.

JEM: Soon's aas finished me toast.
    (*JULE exits.*)

LILY: He's dead then, yer Dad?

BEN: 'Fraid so, Mam.

LILY: Thought I hadn't sin him fer a while.

BEN: Yer'll still go back t' school when it's all ower.

JEM: I wun't.

BEN: Openly insolent – *openly insolent!*

LILY: Report him ter social services, Mags. They'd be on him
    like a ton o' bricks, they would.

BEN: Oh shut up, yer daft ol' bat!

LILY: Divn't yer talk ter your elders like that, you chauvinistic
    bastard!!

BEN: Great – ah'm a chauvinist now!

JEM: Well, 's an improvement on a paedophile.

LILY: He's one o' them an' arl! Ah bet he beats you up, dun't he Mags? Doan't you stand for it!

MAGS: He dun't beat me, Lily. He's never laid a hand on me, ever.

BEN: Wouldn't bloody dare.

LILY: He should be helpin' his family, not abusin' 'em!

BEN: Go an' tek yer Nan out, Jem. Show her the flyin' saucers.

JEM: Aye, cum on Nan. I got summat'll relax yer; get yer bowels movin' an' arl.

LILY: 'S not a radox bath, is it?

JEM: No, 's better than a bath.

LILY: (*Getting up.*) He moved the bathroom, *silly bugger!*

BEN: See yer later, Mam.

LILY: (*Exiting.*) *Pervert!*

(*LILY and JEM exit. BEN looks depressed.*)

MAGS: Cheer up, Ben.

BEN: What?!

MAGS: Things could be worse; 'least we got our health.

BEN: Me own mother wants me locked away.

MAGS: She doan't know what she's sayin'.

BEN: Christ, I look after her; took her in rather than stick her in an 'ome.

MAGS: (*Suddenly serious.*) No Ben – *I* look after her.

(*MAGS exits. BEN waits a while and then opens the door to see if all is clear, then he retrieves a bottle of whisky he's concealed in the kitchen. He swigs it straight from the bottle and sighs, satisfied.*)

BEN: *Ohh, that's better*...that's much better!

(*Music. Lights fade to blackout.*)

# Scene 4

*The cornfield. Afternoon. A few days later. JEM enters, looking for LILY.*

JEM: (*Calling.*) Nan! Nan! You there, Nan...? (*To himself.*) Bloody 'ell, where's she got to now?
> (*DAVE appears at the boundary fence. He has a dressing on his head.*)

DAVE: Well she ain't over 'ere, thank God!

JEM: *Dave!*

DAVE: How goes it, Jem?

JEM: Great Dave, great...! Well no, actually it's crap.

DAVE: Same as usual, then?

JEM: 'Fraid so. Ye're not s'posed ter be near 'ere, Dave.

DAVE: I know, but I thought I'd try an' see Jule; 's bin ages.
> (*Waving a four-pack.*) I got some cans – want one?

JEM: *Do I ever?* We're seriously runnin' short o' booze.

DAVE: So...is it all right?

JEM: Aye, cum over. You en't bin in any infected areas, 'ave yer?

DAVE: Just the barracks.

JEM: Tha's alreet then.
> (*DAVE climbs over the fence.*)

DAVE: The Terminator's on the loose again then?

JEM: Keeps wanderin' off. Found her asleep in JCB bucket yesterday.

DAVE: Dangerous woman.

JEM: Ahh, she's alreet...well most o' the time... (*Concerned.*) How's yer 'ead?

DAVE: A bit sore, still.

JEM: *Shit!*

DAVE: On the mend. Here –
> (*DAVE throws JEM a can. They crack a pair.*)

JEM: *Nice one!* (*Swigs.*) Crikey, I needed tha'!

DAVE: How's Jule?

JEM: Worried. Still can't move cattle 'cause of restrictions.

DAVE: Can't last much longer.

36

JEM: Hope not. 'S like we're all trapped in a microwave, or summat. Dad just shouts all time.

DAVE: Nothin' new there then.

JEM: Tha's fer sure. Ah doan't know what ah'm ganna do when it's all ower; not much use round 'ere really.

DAVE: Takes all sort to make a world.

JEM: What d'yer mean?

DAVE: Well…you, you're interested in other stuff, aren't yer? Like space an' the stars an' stuff.

JEM: (*Points.*) There's our nearest star.

DAVE: It's daytime.

JEM: *Sun,* sun's a star.

DAVE: Oh…yeah. Least some things in life are constant.

JEM: Nowt's constant. Be a red giant one day when it's burnt all its hydrogen up. Earth's atmosphere'll evaporate 'n' then the sun'll explode tekin' rest o' the solar system wi' it.

DAVE: Bit of a drag.

JEM: We'll 'ave populated other worlds by then, so it wun't matter.

DAVE: Like the aliens?

JEM: We're the future aliens.

DAVE: You reckon there really is something out there?

JEM: Gorra be. Gorra be more ter life than this; it dun't mek sense, else. *We* dun't mek sense.

DAVE: Hey, cheer up! Things'll sort themselves out sooner or later.

JEM: Reckon?

DAVE: Yeah. Look at me; I dunno what the future's got in store for me. I can't stay a soldier forever, but what's the point of worryin' about it?

JEM: Yer could be a model.

DAVE: What?

JEM: Yer know, they 'ave male models, dun't they?

DAVE: I'm a soldier, Jem.

JEM: I know, but ye're… Ah dunno, ye're good lookin', like.

DAVE: (*Laughs.*) You wanna be careful; people'll start gettin' the wrong idea about you.

JEM: (*Laughs defensively.*) No, I din't mean 'owt like that.
Bloody 'ell! *I mean…!*

DAVE: Your Dad'd do himself in – *Ben Handley's boy a queer!*

JEM: (*Nervous laugh.*) He wouldn't like that.

DAVE: (*Serious tone.*) You're not, are you?

JEM: (*Shocked, defensive.*) *No!*

DAVE: (*Laughs.*) Only jokin', Jem.

JEM: (*Laughs.*) Aye, I know.

DAVE: You're a man's man, aren't yer?

JEM: I am, aye.

DAVE: Two of a pair, mate!
(*They clink cans together, JEM grins.*)

JEM: *Two of a pair!*
(*They swig a toast. JULE approaches from the house.*)

JULE: (*Calling.*) Nan…! Nan…!

JEM: (*Calls back.*) Ower 'ere, Jule.

JULE: (*Approaching.*) Yer found her?

JEM: No, I found someone else.

JULE: What…? (*Confronts DAVE.*) *What you doin' 'ere?*

DAVE: Come to see you.

JULE: No one's allowed 'ere just yet. I told yer on phone.

DAVE: (*Getting up.*) I'd better go then.

JULE: *No!*

DAVE: Make your mind up, Jule. Do you want me or not?

JULE: 'Course I want yer.

DAVE: Yeah?

JULE: Yeah… *'Course I want yer!*
(*JULE embraces DAVE, desperately. They kiss. JEM moves off apace, but still hangs around, watching.*)

DAVE: I've been missin' you, sweetheart.

JULE: Me too… Oh look at yer 'ead –

DAVE: On the mend… Jule, we're gonna be on the move soon.

JULE: Oh…reet.

DAVE: Just thought you should know.

JULE: Aye…aye thanks.

DAVE: So…?

JULE: What?

DAVE: Oh come on; don't make it difficult for me.

JULE: Is that why ye've cum 'ere?

DAVE: I've come to see you… I want you to come with me; marry me if you like.

JULE: (*Laughs.*) Christ, I dun't believe this!

DAVE: What are you sayin'? Do you love me, or what?

JULE: Climb ower the fence wi' yer ultimatums.

DAVE: I just don't know what you think. Why won't you say? Tell me to piss off if you like.

JULE: Now ye're just talkin' daft.

DAVE: Am I? I feel like I embarrass you or something. You made me hide from your Mum; first time your Dad saw me was on a stretcher!

JEM: She *never* brings her boyfriends back… I mean never in the past…not that she's seein' anybody else, 'cause she en't, Dave. Ye're the on'y one this time, an' ah'd be straight wi' yer, mate; yer know I would… Anyway, er…jest thought ah'd tell yer that.

JULE: You still 'ere? What is it wi' you? It's creepy the way ye're allus spyin' on us.

JEM: Ah wuz just…tryin' to help… I weren't spyin'.

DAVE: We'll be movin' soon, Jule.

JULE: 'N' you expect me ter throw everythin' up on a whim?

JEM: You should go, Jule.

JULE: What?

JEM: God, Jule. I couldn't bear fer yer ter go away. Ye're the on'y one 'ere who really understands me. But you an' Dave…well ah wish somebody loved *me* like that. (*Pause.*)

DAVE: Think it over, eh? Let me know –

JULE: Dave, it's not that easy…it's…

DAVE: (*Climbing the fence.*) Gimme a call, eh?

JULE: Aye…ah'll call yer, I promise… Be careful on that range, wun't yer?

DAVE: (*Laughs.*) Your family's far more dangerous than the range.

(*DAVE exits. JEM is looking at JULE, incredulous.*)

JULE: What you lookin' at?!

JEM: Sorry.

JULE: Allus in the bloody way, you are. What wor yer doin' wi' him, anyroad?

JEM: Sharin' a couple o' cans, tha's arl.

JULE: He'd come ter see me, not you.

JEM: Din't think yer minded.

JULE: Well I do!

JEM: Besides, he's a mate, en't he?

JULE: He en't yer mate, *sad git!*

JEM: He is an' arl.

JULE: Can't yer find mates of yer own age?

JEM: Aye, 'course I can.

JULE: There's summat really unhinged about you.

JEM: 'S alright fer you, but what am ah ganna do? Where am I ganna go?

JULE: One thing I can say is, you stay away from Dave from now on.

JEM: What?

JULE: You 'eard me.

JEM: I en't stayin' away from him.

JULE: I en't askin' yer – ah'm *tellin'* yer.

JEM: I en't ganna stop seein' him.

JULE: (*Smiles.*) Well if yer doan't, ah'm ganna tell him yer wear my lacy panties.

JEM: Yer wouldn't!

JULE: Oh but wouldn't I?

JEM: You…you bloody bitch!

(*JEM throws himself into the corn, sobbing.*)

I wanna die! Ah jest wanna bloody die!

JULE: Oh cum on Jem, pull yerself t'gether – ye're pathetic.

JEM: I know, I know I am – *ah'm pathetic.*

(*MAGS approaches from the house.*)

MAGS: (*Calls.*) Any luck?

JULE: Round 'ere? I doubt it!

MAGS: I wish she wouldn't keep doin' this… (*Notices JEM crying.*) Wha's wrong wi' Jem?

JULE: Who knows?

JEM: *Leave me alone!*

MAGS: Wha's up, Jem?

JEM: Jest leave me alone!

JULE: Oh let him cry.

MAGS: Doan't talk like that, Jule, I know ye're upset, but he's yer brother.

JULE: I en't even sure o' that.

MAGS: What yer talkin' about?

JEM: Shut up! Shut up, you cow! Dun't you say 'owt!

JULE: I wouldn't really say… Jem… I… (*Sighs.*) Oh, ah'd better get back I s'pose; see ter the cows.

MAGS: Yer Dad's doin' the milkin'.

JULE: 'S *my* job – I allus do it. He wun't let me near 'em anymore.

MAGS: Well he wants ter keep an eye on 'em. You can understand that.

JULE: I know 'em better than him; saw 'em into the world.

MAGS: He's jest concerned.

JULE: 'S 'cause ah've got tits, en't it?

MAGS: You lost me there, Jule.

JULE: 'S 'cause I en't a bloody son an' heir.

MAGS: Jule, dun't talk like that…

(*JULE begins to walk off.*)

(*Calls after her.*) Jule…!

(*But JULE ignores her and exits.*)

(*Weary.*) Wha's bin goin' on, Jem? You alreet, son?

JEM: No, I en't. I en't ever ganna be alreet.

MAGS: Yer mustn't talk like that, 'course yer will. Ye're at that funny age, tha's arl.

JEM: En't nuthin' funny about it!

MAGS: It'll pass, Jem, believe me.

JEM: It wun't. 'N' *she* can be nice one minute, next she's a complete bitch!

MAGS: Is it school? Are yer bein' bullied? Is that why yer
    wun't go no more?

JEM: They pick on me.

MAGS: Pick on yer? Why?

JEM: Ah doan't know.

MAGS: C'mon, tell us –

    (*Pause.*)

JEM: 'S 'cause ah'm different.

MAGS: How are yer different?

JEM: Dunno, divn't like football.

MAGS: So?

JEM: Dun't know how ter speak their language; feel
    uncomfortable wi' 'em…get on better wi' girls.

MAGS: 'S 'cause ye're the sensitive type, tha's arl.

JEM: Dad thinks ah'm a waste o' space.

MAGS: No he doesn't.

JEM: Ah should be the farmer, not Jule.

MAGS: Why? Who's ter say it should be that way round?
    Ye're jest a lad findin' his way in world. You'll discover
    what yer wanna do wi' yerself in yer own time.

JEM: Aye?

MAGS: Aye. Look, why dun't yer talk it ower wi' yer Dad?

JEM: Yer must be jokin'!

MAGS: Tell him how yer feel. He en't an ogre.

JEM: Like *yeah!*

MAGS: He's just bin under a lot of pressure, tha's arl. He'd be
    dead chuffed ter think ye'd cum to him wi' yer troubles.

JEM: He's got enough of his own.

MAGS: Jest be honest wi' him. You en't ganna tell him 'owt
    that'll shock him.

JEM: Ah doan't know about that. Mam, I…

MAGS: C'mon let's find yer Nan an' ah'll do us some chips fer tea.

JEM: Okay.

    (*They begin to exit.*)

MAGS: You bin smokin' again, Jem?

JEM: Not jest now, no.

MAGS: I weren't born yesterday. Ah can smell it – *tobacco smoke*.

JEM: I en't, honestly.

MAGS: Pull the other one.

> (*They exit. LILY emerges from the corn with a huge spliff on. She takes a drag, smiles and goes back down again. Music. Lights fade to blackout.*)

## Scene 5

*The house. Morning. MAGS is pouring hot water into the pot. BEN enters from milking.*

BEN: Somebody's bin at the corn again.

MAGS: *Ohh…!*

BEN: En't ganna be any left soon. 'S them bleedin' tin-'eads from the artillery range.

MAGS: We've never had any trouble from 'em before.

BEN: Revenge attack fer Jule's boyfriend.

MAGS: Nowt ter do wi' it.

> (*Pause. MAGS continues making tea.*)

You wor up early again.

BEN: Aye well, yer know…lot ter do.

MAGS: Yer should let Jule do more. She's allus done the milkin'. 'S her herd, really.

BEN: I jest… I gorra keep an eye on things, Mags. Can't afford ter miss 'owt.

MAGS: She knows what ter look fer.

BEN: It's not that I dun't trust her.

MAGS: She wants ter help, tha's arl. We're all pullin' together, so include her, alreet?

BEN: Aye…alreet…

> (*MAGS hands BEN a mug of tea.*)

Ta. Anyway, Mam seems to have calmed down hell of a lot, lately.

MAGS: Jem's influence that is. They're allus t'gether, that pair. One good thing about him bein' at home now.

BEN: S'pose so.

MAGS: He's a good lad, really.

BEN: Aye.

MAGS: Jest needs a bit of encouragement now an' then.

(*Pause.*)

Yer need to 'ave that word wi' him.

BEN: Ah doan't know what ter say.

MAGS: Just tell him…tell him yer love him.

BEN: I en't tellin' him that!

MAGS: He's goin' through summat bad at the moment, ah can sense it.

BEN: We all are.

MAGS: He'd be dead chuffed if yer took an interest.

BEN: Talks such rubbish; winds yer like a clock, he does.

MAGS: He's a lad; that's what lads are supposed ter do.

BEN: No excuse. I mean, what time is it now?

MAGS: He's a teenager – he's lazy. So what?

(*Pause.*)

BEN: He's alreet though…? Ah mean, yer know ah divn't know wha's gannin' on in his head, lately.

MAGS: He's fine, he just needs yer ter tek an interest in him now an' then.

(*JEM enters.*)

JEM: 'Lo!

BEN: *Talk of the livin' dead!* Wha's dragged you from yer stinkin' pit?

JEM: I bin up ages, actually. Checkin' out new corn-circle. Sin it?

BEN: 'S them soddin' tin-'eads!

JEM: It's a sign. Conditions are all cummin' t'gether. Reckon ah'll see 'em soon.

BEN: *Sign?* It's jest flattened corn.

JEM: *Radioactive?*

BEN: How d'yer know that?

JEM: I can feel it.

BEN: (*Scornful.*) *Radioactive!*

MAGS: Ben!

BEN: What?

MAGS: You know. Get on wi' it –

BEN: What?

MAGS: You 'eard me.

(*MAGS begins to exit.*)

BEN: Where yer gannin'?

MAGS: See ter the hens.

BEN: We en't got no hens.

(*MAGS has gone. Pause.*)

JEM: Wha's this then – *fatherly chat?* Should be interestin'.

BEN: (*Sighs.*) How did all this happen, eh?

JEM: All what? Depletion of the ozone-layer, microwaves frazzlin' our brains?

BEN: You an' me.

(*Pause.*)

JEM: Ye've bin busy.

BEN: Ye're me on'y son, Jem. Ah doan't wanna think of yer upset all the time.

JEM: Ah'm alreet.

BEN: Ah can't figure you out. All this alien stuff an' arl. Ye're seventeen years old, en't it about time yer dropped it?

JEM: I sin 'em.

BEN: Yer saw nowt. 'S yer imagination carryin' yer away.

JEM: No it en't. I saw their strange craft at boundary fence; all lights flashin' 'n' stuff.

BEN: Ye'd better pull yerself t'gether, lad, or ye're ganna end up in' loony bin.

JEM: I en't no loony! The voices in me 'ead told me that.

BEN: You 'earin' voices now?

JEM: *Alien voices.* 'S telepathy, en't it?

BEN: What am ah ganna do wi' you?

JEM: They've chosen me.

BEN: Aye, as a perfect example of a twenty-first century earth twat! They'll put you in alien zoo; see yer jabberin' behind bars like a bloody monkey.

JEM: Tha's arl you know! They divn't 'ave bars, they 'ave force-fields.

BEN: Why dun't yer talk it ower wi' doctor? Mebbe yer needs some o' that *prozac* stuff.

JEM: I got all the drugs ah need, thanks.

BEN: Ye're on drugs, an' arl?!

JEM: Jus' soft stuff, dope mainly.

BEN: Ah divn't wanna know… *Dope?* Wha's goin' on, Jem? What is wrong wi' you?

JEM: Can ah be honest?

BEN: Ah'm yer Dad, 'course yer can be honest. Cum on – spit it out.

JEM: Aas in the wrong body.

BEN: 'S the same body you allus had. You have *not* bin abducted by aliens.

JEM: Aas in wrong body, Dad. Ah mean it.

BEN: An' so do I. You 'ave not bin replaced by a bloody replicant.

JEM: Yer doan't understand, Dad. What ah mean is: ah'm in a man's body.

BEN: (*Correcting.*) Boy's body.

JEM: Okay – *boy's body.* It's still the wrong body.

BEN: 'S the on'y one yer got.

JEM: Tha's the trouble.

BEN: What yer rabbitin' on about, lad?

JEM: I'm in a…*boy's body.*

BEN: Aye?

JEM: But ah should be in a girl's body.

BEN: (*Laughs.*) Plenty o' time for arl that! Go up town a bit more; get yer sister t' tek yer ter one o' them clubs she goes to.

JEM: I should be in a *girl's* body.

BEN: I know. I was jest the same when I wor your age.

JEM: *You?!*

BEN: Ah doan't sound so surprised. I loved messin' about 'afore I met yer Mam.

JEM: Really?

BEN: Oh aye, looked a picture I did them days.

JEM: *Wow.....!* Well, 's normal then?

BEN: 'Course it's normal. Nowt wrong wi' messin' about a bit.

JEM: (*Relieved.*) *Oh Dad!*

BEN: Is that all ye're worried about?

JEM: Well...

BEN: Yer daft sod. You mess about all yer like. All men do.

JEM: Do they?!

BEN: Till yer settle down, like.

JEM: Then yer stop?

BEN: Have too, lad. Can't have it interferin' wi' yer marriage.

JEM: I doan't think I *could* stop.

BEN: Yer will when yer meet the right girl.

JEM: No – I *wun't.*

BEN: (*Laughs.*) Yer will! Doan't look so serious; 's nowt ter
worry about.

JEM: (*Smiles.*) Thanks Dad.

BEN: (*Ruffles his hair.*) *Chip off the old block!*

JEM: Can't imagine you in a dress, though.

BEN: *What?*

LILY: (*Off.*) *You shouldna' waked me!*

MAGS: (*Off.*) Yer wor cold as ice.

(*MAGS and LILY enter.*)

LILY: I wor 'avin' a lovely dream, I were.

MAGS: Ah couldn't leave yer there, Lily... (*To BEN.*) Sorry
– yer finished?

BEN: Er...I think so. Wha's up now?

MAGS: Found her asleep in JCB bucket again. Ah reckon
she's bin there all night.

BEN: Why'd yer do that, Mam?

LILY: Why did *you* move my room?!

BEN: If ye're confused jest cum an' get us.

LILY: First the bathroom...!

JEM: Ah'll get her a hot drink, shall I?

LILY: ...then my bloody bedroom!

MAGS: Good lad – there's tea in' pot...

LILY: Ah divn't know what yer think ye're playin' at, ah really dun't. It's cruel!

BEN: Ah din't move yer room.

LILY: Ah'm freezin', I am…cold ter me bones.

MAGS: Sit yerself down, Lily –

(*MAGS helps LILY to the sofa.*)

LILY: Had a lovely dream, ah did.

MAGS: Tha's nice.

BEN: Ah doan't know what we're ganna do; I really doan't.

LILY: Yer Dad wor alive, Bernard.

BEN: He's dead, Mam; ye've gorra believe me.

LILY: I know that! Think ah'm stupid? I meant he wor alive in me dream.

BEN: Oh…

LILY: Think ah'm stupid?

JEM: (*With mug.*) Drink that, Nan –

LILY: Nice cup o' tea – lovely. Just what ah need. 'S bloody cold in that barn.

BEN: If yer can't find yer room, *or anythin'* – cum an' tell us.

LILY: I can never find yer. (*Sips mug.*) Tha's better! Good lad, he is; looks after his old Nan, he does.

JEM: No problemo!

LILY: *Ooh, ah'm warmin' up now…*saw Jack, ah did. You look just like him, Bernard.

BEN: (*Smiles.*) Do I, Mam?

LILY: Handsome man he wuz. Loved this place, he did. You tek care on it, Bernard – 's yourn now.

BEN: Aye…ah'll do me best, Mam.

LILY: Ah know yer will. (*Sips tea.*)

MAGS: Got the colour back in yer cheeks now.

(*JULE enters. She shoots BEN a look.*)

JULE: Done the milkin' ah see?

BEN: Aye.

JULE: Bit early, weren't it?

BEN: Things is different at the moment.

JULE: Yer can say that again.

MAGS: Where've yer bin?

JULE: Spread some straw out in' meadow – 's a reet mess.

BEN: They should let us move 'em now.

JULE: Yer reckon?

BEN: More corn gone.

JULE: I saw.

LILY: 'Ey, remember when we used ter cut the corn?

BEN: What?

LILY: Long time ago when yer wor a nipper?

BEN: Oh…aye.

LILY: 'Fore we had the big machines.

BEN: Were I born then?

LILY: 'Course you wor born. Used ter have a few labourers then: Barry Braithwaite an' whasisname? Terry… Terry…

BEN: *Bailey.* Terry Bailey.

LILY: Him an' arl, aye. An' some o' the others'd cum from down road an' a couple from town; bring their kids an' arl.

BEN: (*Smiles.*) Oh, tha's reet, I remember.

LILY: 'Course yer remember. Yer used t' play wi' 'em. We caught you arl wi' no clothes on.

JEM: What?

BEN: What yer talkin' about, Mam?

LILY: You an' the Jenkins kids runnin' through corn like little pink grubs.

BEN: I can't remember that.

MAGS: Go on, Lily – I wanna 'ear more about this.

BEN: I wuz never naked. Ah've never bin naked.

JEM: Well yer must've bin at least twice.

LILY: Three years old yer were.

BEN: Oh well – *three years old!*

LILY: Runnin' through corn like little pink grubs. An' we'd all set about it t'gether – proper haystacks, then.

BEN: I can barely remember.

LILY: We'd work all day; start really early, 'n we'd have us home-med boiled ham.

BEN: Ah remember that. Ooh that wor lovely, that were – thick as a plate.

LILY: Home-med boiled ham an' bread an' butter an' yer uncle Graham's tomatoes. An' when we'd finished we'd crack open cider; drink it in fields.

BEN: Tha's reet – *cider!*

LILY: Yer Dad used ter brew it.

MAGS: We still got the old press somewhere.

BEN: 'S in the barn, up in loft.

JEM: Ah love cider. We should brew some again.

LILY: What fer?

JEM: Well…ter drink, Nan.

LILY: No, 's for the labourers; 's fer when we gets the corn in.

JEM: We en't got no labourers.

BEN: No, we got bloody aliens now.

LILY: Well they en't havin' none – 's fer the workers.

MAGS: Sounds lovely, Lily.

LILY: Oh it were, Mags. I used ter love hay-makin'.

BEN: An' now hay's rottin' in' fields all ower England.

MAGS: Things were uncomplicated then.

LILY: Were they?

MAGS: Sounds like it ter me.

LILY: Ah divn't know 'owt about that.

MAGS: Well yer know, everybody lendin' a hand, gerrin' stuck in, like.

LILY: What with?

JEM: Hay-makin', Nan.

LILY: Doan't talk ter me about hay-makin'!

JEM: But yer jest said…

LILY: Break yer bloody back it did.

MAGS: But you had boiled ham an' cider.

LILY: Worst time o' the year; used ter dread it, we did. No big machines then.

(*Pause.*)

JULE: Know where else ah've bin?

MAGS: Where yer bin, Jule?

JULE: I went ower ter the shed; thought ah'd look ower the
    herd… They got it en't they?

BEN: (*Quietly.*) Aye.

JULE: You knew.

BEN: Known fer a while.

JULE: Tha's why yer wouldn't let me near 'em.

BEN: (*Nods.*) Tha's why.

MAGS: Ohh…! *Oh crikey!*

JULE: Why din't yer say?

BEN: They shouldn't be able t' kill 'em like they do – it en't reet.
    (*MAGS embraces him.*)
    It en't reet, Mags.

MAGS: Ah know.
    (*Music. Lights fade to blackout.*)

# Scene 6

*Three days later. The house. MAGS, BEN, JEM and LILY are there.*
*There is the sound of cows mooing coming from outside. Suddenly a few*
*gunshots ring out too. There is a half empty bottle of whisky on the table.*
*BEN is half-cut.*

BEN: Ah should be out there.

MAGS: Jule's there.

BEN: I shouldn't leave it to her.

JEM: She looked terrible.

BEN: Ah should be there an' arl.

MAGS: Be ower soon.

BEN: Anyway, 's *her* boyfriend doin' the shootin' en't it?

JEM: What difference does that mek?

BEN: Army bastard!

LILY: *Army bastard!*

JEM: He's just follerin' orders.

BEN: Whose side you on?

JEM: It en't about sides, is it?

BEN: Whose side is he on, eh?

MAGS: Cum on, love…hold on, eh?

BEN: Aye…'s hard though.

(*Gun shots ring out.*)

*Bastards!* (*Almost crying.*) *Bastards!*

(*MAGS offers her hand, but BEN grabs the whisky bottle and pours a glass.*)

The whole bloody herd.

LILY: What's wrong wi' Bernard?

MAGS: He's upset, Lily.

LILY: Wha's wrong, Bernard?

BEN: Nowt Mam.

LILY: Yer divn't look very well.

BEN: Aye, ah'm…a bit under the weather.

LILY: Get yer some herbal relaxation. That'll sort him out, wun't it Jem?

JEM: Er…yeah.

BEN: Wha's she talkin' about?

JEM: (*Shrugs.*) Ah doan't know.

(*More shots ring out.*)

LILY: Army bastards! Ah cracked his head open! (*Laughs.*)

MAGS: We know yer did, Lily.

BEN: Never thought ah'd see the day.

MAGS: Get the compensation, though.

BEN: 'S my time an' sweat's gone inter rearin' 'em.

MAGS: 'S a good package so I hear. Yer can get money fer cleanin' up an' arl. Some farmers are mekin' a packet out on it.

BEN: 'Ten't reet though, is it?

MAGS: Mebbe not, but we'd be daft not ter tek advantage of it.

BEN: I built up that herd, I did.

JEM: An' Jule.

BEN: 'S me who's responsible for 'em.

JEM: How come you en't out there then?

BEN: *You little bastard!*

(*BEN lashes out at JEM with a back-hander. It sends JEM flying across the room. Everyone is shocked.*)

MAGS: *What yer doin'?!* En't no need fer that.

BEN: Well…why's he tauntin' me then? Windin' me up at a time like this?

JEM: (*On the verge of tears.*) Ah'm allus sayin' the wrong thing, I am.

MAGS: You alreet, Jem?

JEM: Aye, ah'm fine.

LILY: Ah'm ganna report you, I am.

BEN: *Oh Christ…!* (*Swigs bottle.*)

MAGS: Leave that alone now, Ben. That en't gun'ter help.

BEN: 'S the *on'y* thing that does help.

(*The shooting continues.*)

LILY: Wha's all that noise out there?

JEM: Yer divn't wanna know, Nan.

LILY: Wha's gannin' on?

MAGS: Nowt fer you ter worry about, Lily.

BEN: Oh tell her. She'll find out sooner or later.

MAGS: This en't the time.

BEN: The army are shootin' our cattle.

JEM: *Oh great!*

MAGS: Feel better now?

BEN: 'S the truth, en't it?

LILY: *The army are shootin' our cattle?!*

MAGS: Now doan't upset yerself, Lily.

LILY: Well yer gorra do summat about it, Bernard.

JEM: Nowt we *can* do, Nan.

LILY: Yer can't let 'em kill our herd!

BEN: They can do what they want. The world's turned upside down.

MAGS: 'S foot an' mouth, Lily.

LILY: Ah like the cows.

BEN: I know yer does, Mam.

LILY: Ah like 'em.

BEN: Well they're off ter the great abattoir in the sky now.

MAGS: Ye're not bein' helpful 'ere, Ben.

LILY: They got foot an' mouth?

MAGS: Ministry says we gorra 'ave 'em culled, Lily.

LILY: Foot an' mouth on my farm? Din't yer tek precautions?

BEN: I did all ah could, Mam.

LILY: Your Dad'll turn in his grave, he will.

BEN: Ah know.

LILY: He wouldn've let this happen.

MAGS: It's all ower the country, Lily.

LILY: That's no excuse! Ye're bloody useless you are!

BEN: Ah know.

LILY: Bloody useless! *Army are killin' our cattle?!* Your Dad'll
turn in his grave.

JEM: Calm down now, Nan.

(*JEM helps her to the sofa.*)

LILY: *Turn in his grave!* (*Crying quietly.*)

JEM: Relax Nan, it'll all be ower soon.

(*More shooting. JULE enters. She looks very upset.*)

JULE: I can't watch no more…it's horrible! (*Cries.*)

(*MAGS embraces her.*)

It's horrible, Mam. They're all lyin' on ground – it's
horrible, it is!

MAGS: Ah know.

BEN: Thanks lass.

JULE: What fer?

BEN: Bein' there; doin' what ah should be doin'.

JULE: Aye well…somebody's gorra line 'em up, en't they?

BEN: Oh, doan't be like that. Ah would if ah could.

LILY: They got foot an' mouth, en't they Julie?

JULE: Yer told her then?

MAGS: It slipped out.

LILY: They're shootin' 'em; tha's what the noise is…*ah'm ever
so upset.*

JULE: Me too… Should see it out there – all pilin' up at side
o' barn…blood all ower the yard.

LILY: Wha's goin' on wi' this farm?

(*The doorbell rings.*)

MAGS: Get it, will yer Jem.

(*JEM exits.*)

BEN: That'll be me curry.

JULE: Ye've ordered a curry?!

BEN: Well ah dun't care about quarantine restrictions
anymore.

JULE: Piles o' carcasses out there an' ye've ordered a curry?!

BEN: I en't had one in ower a month. Gorra eat en't yer?

(*JEM enters with DAVE.*)

JEM: 'S Dave.

DAVE: Hope you don't mind. I saw Jule was upset. Sergeant
said I could call in.

(*JULE embraces him.*)

JULE: Aww thanks babe!

BEN: Enjoyin' yerself, *babe?* Slaughterin' my cattle?

DAVE: 'Course I'm not enjoyin' it.

MAGS: You pack that in reet now!

JULE: What is your problem?

LILY: (*Suddenly.*) *It's him!* He's the one who raped Julie in' corn!

JEM: He weren't rapin' her; she liked it.

BEN *In broad bloody daylight!*

MAGS: Do yer wanna a drink, Dave?

BEN: He en't havin' my whisky!

MAGS: I meant a cup of tea.

DAVE: I know you must be feelin' bad right now.

BEN: (*Laughs.*) Hark at him: waltzes in 'ere wi' blood on his
hands; all fine words an' sympathy.

DAVE: I'm just tryin' to be civil.

JULE: (*To BEN.*) Yer need treatment, you do!

MAGS: I think yer should leave that whisky alone now.

BEN: If I can't have a drink at a time like this…

MAGS: Do yer want a cup of tea, Dave?

DAVE: No thanks. I can't stay long.

(*More gunshots. Pause.*)

BEN: Many left?

DAVE: Not many… We're bein' as humane as possible. None
of 'em are sufferin'.

BEN: Really? Thought ye'd be glad of a bit o' target practice.

JULE: Ignore him, Dave.

JEM: Everybody else does.

(*BEN lifts his fist.*)

BEN: *Ah'll bloody –*

JEM: Go on then – if it helps.

BEN: Sorry, ah…ah dunno…sorry for earlier an' arl, Jem.

JEM: Sure.

BEN: (*To DAVE.*) I know what ye're thinkin'…

MAGS: Ben, why doan't yer just sit down an' have a cup of coffee an' try an' relax?

BEN: … Think we all run around in Land Rover Discoveries, dun't yer?

DAVE: Not at all.

BEN: Big bull bars speedin' down country lanes, shoutin', *'get off my land!'* Kids at young farmers' balls, holiday villa in France; creamin' off the fat o' the land.

DAVE: I know it's not like that.

BEN: *Aye?* Well it *is* like that…!

JULE: (*Pissed off.*) *Christ!*

BEN: …*Fer some:* fer the rich landed gentry wi' acres an' acres of estates, racehorses an' big houses. But not fer the likes of us bein' screwed by the supermarkets, regulations, prices at market gerrin' lower an' lower…

MAGS: Alreet now, Ben…

(*JEM suddenly notices LILY has picked up DAVE's gun and is pointing it at him.*)

JEM: What yer doin' wi' the gun, Nan?

BEN: Mam, put it down.

MAGS: Gie it 'ere Lily, dun't be rash.

LILY: *Bollocks!* Ah'm ganna put a bullet in the murderin' bastard!

BEN: Now, now, Mam; tha's not a good idea.

DAVE: It's all right – the safety catch is on.

(*LILY flips the safety catch.*)

LILY: *Army bastard!*

JEM: *Oh shit!*

(*LILY fires the gun, but it just clicks.*)

DAVE: An' it's not loaded anyway.

JULE: *Bloody hell!*

JEM: (*Taking the gun from her.*) Ah'll tek that, Nan –

BEN: Ah doan't believe it! Yer nearly murdered him!

LILY: Tha's what yer want, en't it?

    (*BEN swigs his bottle. The doorbell rings. JEM goes.*)

MAGS: Dun't let anybody else in jest now, reet?

JEM: Who'd wanna cum in 'ere, anyroad?

BEN: She wor gonna kill him – *Christ!*

DAVE: Well there's no harm done.

JULE: Ah'm sorry about all this, Dave.

DAVE: No worries.

BEN: (*Explaining.*) My Mam...she's...

LILY: *She's what?*

BEN: She's...my Mam.

LILY: Talk sense, yer bloody pervert!

    (*JEM enters with a take-away curry.*)

JEM: 'S yer curry.

    (*BEN takes it.*)

BEN: It stinks!

JEM: He saw the cows bein' slaughtered.

BEN: So?

JEM: He wor sick...in' bag.

    (*Pause. BEN drops the bag in the bin.*)

    He's at the door – 's nine fifty.

BEN: (*Exiting.*) Ever had one o' them days when nowt seems
    ter go reet?

    (*BEN exits.*)

LILY: Where's Bernard gone?

JEM: Ter pay fer the curry he's just chucked in' bin.

LILY: He needs ter see a psychiatrist.

MAGS: Jem, tek yer Nan fer a lie down.

JEM: Aye, good idea. Cum on Nan –

LILY: Aye, le's chill out, eh Jem?

JEM: Er...yeah.

    (*JEM smiles at the puzzled looks as they exit.*)

MAGS: Look ah'll leave you two alone fer a while. You en't sin each other for some time 'ave yer?

JULE: Thanks Mam.

DAVE: Nice t' meet you, Mrs Handley.

MAGS: She's a good girl, our Jule.

DAVE: I know that.

MAGS: I dun't know why I said that… I…well ah'm sure ye'll both work it all out t'gether.

JULE: *Mam –*

MAGS: Aye, ah'm goin'.

(*MAGS exits.*)

JULE: Welcome ter the family.

DAVE: Thanks. I wish it could have been…*better.*

(*They laugh and go to kiss. But something stops JULE.*)

JULE: There's some blood on yer face.

DAVE: Oh…sorry.

(*She wipes it away for him.*)

JULE: Can't be helped – it's everywhere.

DAVE: Yeah…it is… You okay?

JULE: Ohh…ah dunno, 's bloody hard seein' 'em all shot like that.

DAVE: I saw you cryin'… I just wanted to hold you.

JULE: (*Hugs him.*) *Aww babe!*

DAVE: What you gonna do now?

JULE: Hadn't thought. Tek the compensation ah s'pose. Everybody else is. Mebbe when it's all ower we can start up again…hadn't thought that far.

DAVE: I got a definite posting now.

JULE: Have yer?

DAVE: Cyprus.

JULE: Cyprus, eh?

DAVE: Beautiful island: sun, sea…

JULE: Sex?

DAVE: (*Laughs.*) If yer like.

(*Pause.*)

It's big decision time, darlin'.

JULE: *Shit!*

DAVE: Yeah – *shit.*

JULE: Oh bollocks!

DAVE: Them an' all.

JULE: Aas a farmer, Dave. Ah got dirt under me fingernails; 's in me blood.

DAVE: Tha's it then?

JULE: Ah doan't know what ter say.

DAVE: Say you'll come with me.

(*Pause.*)

JULE: I can't.

DAVE: That's that then.

JULE: Oh Dave, I…

(*More shots ring out.*)

DAVE: I'll have to get back or the Sergeant…

(*DAVE begins to exit.*)

JULE: Ah'm sorry, Dave.

DAVE: Yeah, me too.

(*DAVE exits. JULE sits at the table, dismayed. More shots mixed with mooing of cows make her cover her ears with her hands and close her eyes to blot it all out. The sound grows in intensity as the lights fade to blackout.*)

# ACT TWO

## Scene 1

*The house. A week later. It is late morning. MAGS and JULE enter in earnest conversation.*

MAGS: Well...p'raps yer should call him, talk things ower?

JULE: *No way!* Besides I en't heard from him fer ages.

MAGS: He'll be gone soon though, Jule. Then it'll be too late.

JULE: Ah've med me mind up, 's not up ter you.

MAGS: Ah know that.

JULE: *So stop puttin' pressure on me!*

MAGS: Ah'm not, 'course ah'm not.

JULE: Ah got stuff ter do, Mam. I gorra get this farm up an' workin' again.

MAGS: We can all manage farm if yer wanna... I mean if yer really want to...?

JULE: Dun't yer understand? Ah'm a farmer, Mam, it's all ah know; 's all I ever wanted ter do. I was the on'y girl in our class at agricultural college.

MAGS: Ah know yer was.

JULE: Ah can't just throw it all up like that... I can turn this place round, ah know I can. An' now's the ideal time ter change. If we went entirely organic, we'd clean up, I know we would. I wanna be the first female farmer round 'ere; show 'em how ter do it. I can, Mam, ah know I can!

MAGS: If tha's what yer want, love.

JULE: I wish... I wish ah'd met Dave some other time; wish he weren' in the army...wish he weren' goin' away, *the bloody awkward swine!*

*(MAGS embraces JULE, who is clearly upset.)*

MAGS: Why doan't yer call him?

JULE: Will yer stop gannin on at me! I'm gun'ter get me life t'gether properly now, get organised. I wanna get on wi' plannin' the new herd an' stuff; order seed fer next year an' arl. But Dad jest wun't bloody listen. We gorra get on wi' it, 'fore we know it winter'll be on us an' we'll have no crops planned at arl!

MAGS: He's bin wrapped up in things, Jule. The epidemic's hurt him really bad.

JULE: *Stop keep stickin' up for him!* 'S affected all on us. How d'yer think I felt watchin'…watchin…? An' then havin' ter put up wi' sight on 'em slowly rottin' ter pieces all piled up at side o' barn – how dare bloody MAFF go on about health risks!

MAGS: Well they took 'em away now.

JULE: Aye, a week after they were shot! Still stinks to high heaven out there; on'y so much disinfectant can cover up.

BEN: (*Off.*) Get *in there – go on!!*
(*BEN pushes JEM into the room. JEM is holding his sweater tight against him. He looks terrified.*)

MAGS: Why does this family allus 'ave to enter a room like they're declarin' war?

BEN: Look who I just caught climbin' up the barn –

MAGS: What wor yer doin' climbin' up the barn, Jem?

JEM: I like it up there.

MAGS: Well no harm's done, is it? He din't fall or 'owt.

BEN: Ah med him cum down.

MAGS: Ben, am ah missin' summat 'ere?

BEN: His sweater snagged on down-pipe.

MAGS: Well ah'll stitch it up.

BEN: Show 'em –

JEM: *No…no, please Dad, no…?*

BEN: Show 'em yer bloody pervert!

MAGS: Wha's gannin' on?
(*BEN wrestles JEM's hands away and pulls his sweater off – JEM is wearing a bra. He wraps his arms around him, pathetically trying to hide it.*)

JEM: No, please? Leave me alone, Dad!

BEN: He's wearin' a bra! *He's wearin' a fuckin' bra!*

JULE: I thought I told yer ter keep out me drawers?

BEN: *Your drawers?* He's done it before?!

(*JULE leaps up and grabs at her bra.*)

JULE: Gimme me bra back!

JEM: Leave me alone! *Please?!*

MAGS: Let him be!! Tha's enough!

JULE: (*Still tugging.*) I want me bra back, yer bloody weirdo!

JEM: Ah'm sorry, Jule; I din't think ye'd mind.

JULE: I gid yer the knickers, en't that enough?!

BEN: You gid him yer knickers?! *Why?!*

MAGS: Will you let him alone?!

(*MAGS pulls JULE off JEM. JEM, distraught, buries his face in his arms.*)

BEN: Will someone please tell me what's 'appenin' 'ere? Why is Jem wearin' a bra?

JULE: He wants ter be a girl.

BEN: *He what?!*

JEM: But *you* used ter wear women's clothes, Dad.

BEN: Yer what?!

JULE: Tha's where he gets it from then!

BEN: I en't never wore women's clothes!

MAGS: It doan't matter if yer did.

BEN: But I din't!

JULE: 'Least he's honest about it.

BEN: He must've got hold o' wrong end o' stick.

JULE: Tha's an understatement.

JEM: He told me he did; 'afore he met me Mam, like.

BEN: I din't!

JULE: Tek it off!

JEM: What – *now?*

MAGS: Ohh…leave him alone, Jule.

JULE: It's mine! *Tek it off!!*

(*JEM struggles with the fastener, mortified and tearful.*)

JEM: I can't… I can't get it.

MAGS: Oh cum 'ere –

(*MAGS unfastens it, and hands the bra back to JULE.*)

JULE: (*Snatches it.*) An' doan't you *ever* go in my room again
    – understand?!
JEM: (*Nods.*)
BEN: I en't no bloody pervert!
JULE: (*To JEM.*) You sad, sad git!
JEM: *This en't 'appenin'! It en't 'appenin'!*
    (*MAGS helps JEM back into his sweater.*)
BEN: See *me* wearin' women's bras! No bloody way!
LILY: (*Off.*) *Where are they?!*
BEN: Oh Christ…! What is it now?
LILY: (*Off.*) *Bernard!!*
    (*LILY enters.*)
    You bastard!!
BEN: Mornin' Mam.
LILY: Doan't you *mornin' me,* you paedophile!
MAGS: Wha's the trouble, Lily?
LILY: Ah've just bin outside first time in six months.
MAGS: It en't bin that long, Lily. 'S bin a week, tha's arl.
LILY: *Kept me in fer six months!* Where's all the cows gone?
BEN: They've gone, Mam.
LILY: Ah can see that! Where to?
BEN: Calm down Mam, ye're gerrin' confused.
LILY: Why?
BEN: Well, 's the disease, en't it?
LILY: I gorra disease?
BEN: (*Spelling it out.*) 'S the foot an' mouth – I told yer, remember?
LILY: (*Shocked.*) I got foot an' mouth?
BEN: No – the cows.
LILY: Where are they?
BEN: Gone for slaughter.
LILY: They're *dairy cows!*
BEN: (*Spelling it out.*) It were *foot an' mouth.*
LILY: (*Shocked.*) I got foot an' mouth disease?
BEN: Not you.
LILY: Who?
BEN: Christ… I'm trapped in a bloody time-loop!

MAGS: You en't got a disease – the cows have, *did*. They had ter be slaughtered.

LILY: (*To BEN.*) Ye're bloody useless! You need a kick up the arse!

JEM: Sit down Nan –

(*JEM helps LILY to a chair.*)

LILY: (*Sitting.*) Where are the cows?

BEN: (*Shouts.*) *Hitchin a lift up the A595!!*

LILY: No need fer that; no need fer sarcasm.

BEN: Aas sorry, Mam.

LILY: Just 'cause ah'm gerrin' on a bit.

BEN: Aas sorry.

LILY: Ah'll crack your head an' arl, I will; jest like Julie's soldier.

MAGS: Alreet now, Lily –

BEN: Well he's long gone, thank God.

LILY: I saw him again ah did.

BEN: Aye, we all did – shootin' cows in our yard.

LILY: No – before that.

BEN: What? Where? Where did yer see him?

LILY: Same place – in corn, weren' he Jem?

JEM: *Nan* –

BEN: *After* we sealed the farm?

JEM: Nan, I doan't think…

BEN: Shut it you! *After* we sealed the farm?

LILY: Same place. Sniffin' after our Julie he were, dirty swine!

BEN: *Bloody hell!*

MAGS: Now doan't get jumpin' ter conclusions…

BEN: 'S obvious, en't it?

MAGS: You think before you open yer mouth…

BEN: You stupid girl!

JULE: Dad…it wor just at boundary fence; he din't cum any nearer than that. He din't bring it 'ere.

BEN: How d'you know? He were there after restrictions were in place. *You little slag!*

MAGS: How dare yer speak ter yer daughter like that.

BEN: *Sex bloody mad!*

JEM: He hadn't bin near any infected areas.

BEN: You knew an' arl? You…you girly bloody pathetic…
Bloody *thing!*

JULE: It's *you* who told him it was alreet ter wear women's
clothes!

LILY: Jem wears women's clothes?!

JULE: An' Dad.

LILY: Bernard wears women's clothes – *why?*

BEN: Ah doan't wear women's clothes.

JEM: Yer told me yer did, Dad.

BEN: Dun't you mek me out ter be a girly, you soddin' freak!
(*BEN whacks JEM quite violently. Pause.*)
Let that be a lesson… You gorra see a doctor, you have.

MAGS: Leave him alone. Ye've done enough harm.

BEN: I mean it. I want him ter get ter doctor; see if there's any
kind of treatment ter mek him normal.

MAGS: Will yer stop it now?!

JULE: (*Holds her bra up to JEM.*) Here Jem, yer can have it.

JEM: No, ah doan't want it… I wanna be normal.

JULE: (*Rises.*) You are normal. 'S *him* who's fucked up.
(*JULE exits.*)

LILY: Ah divn't like arl this shoutin'. It's upsettin' me. You
shouldn't shout all the time, Bernard; not in front of an old
woman; not in front of yer Mam.

BEN: They drive me to it, Mam. Honestly ah do me best.

LILY: Ah need some herbal relaxation, Jem.

JEM: Later Nan.

BEN: What is it wi' you two? What is this *herbal relaxation…?*
Oh, I get it! *You bloody…!*

LILY: Shut up! All yer does is shout at people, you horrible
man! I din't raise you ter shout at people an' welt yer son.

BEN: He's bin giein' yer drugs, Mam. 'S bloody marijuana, or
pot or summat.

LILY: 'S my herbal relaxation.

BEN: Yer can go ter prison fer it.

LILY: (*Upset.*) Ah'm goin' ter prison?

MAGS: Ye're not goin' ter prison, Lily.

LILY: He said ah were.

BEN: Yer *could* go t' prison.

LILY: Ah divn't wanna go t' prison...!

JEM: (*Screams.*) *Stop it! Stop it! Leave her alone...!*

(*JEM picks up a knife from the table and threatens his dad.*)

(*Crying.*) I hate you! I bloody hate you!

(*JEM throws the knife down and runs from the room.*)

BEN: Get him to a doctor; he needs ter be sorted – see that? Yer bloody see that?

LILY: Mags...?

MAGS: What is it, Lily?

LILY: Ah wanna lie down...ah'm tired.

(*MAGS helps her up.*)

BEN: Aye...you have a lie down, Mam. Ye'll feel much better after a lie down.

MAGS: Cum on, Lily. Ye'll be alreet.

LILY: Ah doan't like all this shoutin'...

BEN: Little nap, Mam; do yer a power of good.

LILY: ...it upsets me.

MAGS: Ah know.

(*LILY and MAGS exit. BEN is alone. He swigs his whisky. He slams his fist on the table.*)

BEN: *What a family...what a bloody family!!*

(*He sits at the table and breaks down. Music. Lights fade to blackout.*)

## Scene 2

*The cornfield. A week later. Twilight. JEM and LILY are sitting at the boundary fence watching the stars come out, sharing a spliff and a couple of cans.*

LILY: Ah miss the cows.

JEM: Me too.

LILY: 'S quiet up 'ere wi'out 'em.

JEM: Aye.

LILY: Seems ever so quiet.

JEM: 'S bin quiet wi'out Jule, I know that.

LILY: Well she's back now.

JEM: *Doan't I know it!*

LILY: She divn't look herself, mind.

JEM: Sounds it though. Bloody moodier than ever, she is.

LILY: Where's she bin?

JEM: Who knows? Said she was off ter see Aunt Dot, but she
died three years ago.

LILY: *Dot's dead?*

JEM: You know that, Nan.

LILY: Aw, poor old Dot.

JEM: Three years ago.

LILY: I din't know.

JEM: Yer must've forgot.

LILY: I keep fergettin' things, yer know.

JEM: Do yer?

LILY: Aye, it worries me.

JEM: Ah shouldn't worry about it.

LILY: No?

JEM: No, 's nowt ter worry about. Sometimes it's good ter
forget stuff, anyroad. 'Specially round 'ere.
(*Pause.*)

LILY: *Poor old Dot…* Fergot me own 'usband died, yer know that?

JEM: 'S easily done.

LILY: How could I ferget that? I hope I en't goin' barmy.

JEM: 'Course you en't.
(*Pause.*)

LILY: I hope I en't got that…

JEM: What?

LILY: Yer know – *alka-seltzer.*

JEM: What?

LILY: No, not alka-seltzer. Wha's the name?

JEM: I shouldn't worry.

LILY: Alka… Alsa… *Elbow?*

JEM: Nowt wrong wi' yer, Nan.

67

LILY: Ah can't remember… Ah'm losin' me bloody marbles, I am.

JEM: No ye're not.

LILY: *Alzheimer's!*

(*Pause.*)

Aye – tha's the one… Aye, I reckon ah've got that.

(*Pause.*)

*Bloody Alzheimer's!*

JEM: No Nan, you en't got Alzheimer's.

LILY: Divn't lie ter me, little 'n'. I allus counted on you. Doan't lie ter me now, Jem; ah couldn't tek it.

JEM: But you en't, Nan.

LILY: Well what is it then? What have ah got?

JEM: Well…yer got – *alka-seltzer!*

(*They both laugh.*)

LILY: Ye're as barmy as me, you are!

JEM: (*Laughs.*) You got alka-seltzer!

LILY: (*Laughs.*) Bloody barmy!

JEM: There's no known cure. Yer just fizz t' death.

LILY: (*Laughs loud and long.*) *Fizz t' death!* (*Laughs.*) You barmy bugger, you! *I got alka-selter!* (*Laughs.*)

(*They are both laughing. Eventually the laughter peters out. JEM passes the spliff back and LILY takes a huge satisfying toke. She is enjoying herself.*)

JEM: Nan –

LILY: Aye?

JEM: Can ah tell yer summat?

LILY: If yer like.

JEM: Yer know the crop-circles?

LILY: *Reet bloody mess!*

JEM: Aye…well…it wor me.

LILY: Ah know that. Ah saw yer doin' it. Wi' a plank an' some rope, were'n it?

JEM: *Aye it were!* How…ah mean when did yer see me, like?

LILY: Ah go walkin' on a night sometime – ah saw yer.

JEM: Yer never said 'owt.

LILY: Ah s'pose yer must 'ave a reason, like.

(*Pause.*)

JEM: They're beautiful yer know. Nobody notices. They jest see the corn all flat. But if yer get above 'em...well the pattern they mek...*wi' the moon shinin' on 'em an' arl...!* Ah used ter climb on roof o' barn ter look. I want *them* ter see it. Ah want 'em ter notice me.

LILY: Who?

JEM: The aliens. Ah want 'em ter cum 'ere an' tek me away wi' 'em. Ah dun't belong 'ere.

LILY: Well what yer doin' 'ere, then?

JEM: 'S me 'ome.

LILY: Dun't 'ave ter be if yer doan't like it. There's plenty of other places in world.

JEM: Ah wuz thinkin' more of another planet.

LILY: Another planet? Ah can't see it 'appenin' meself.

JEM: No.

LILY: If ye're not happy 'ere – bugger off somewhere else. We on'y live once.

JEM: Ah couldn't live anywhere else. Ah couldn't.

LILY: Then leave the field alone – it looks like a fuckin' collander!

JEM: Yer...yer wun't tell anyone, will yer Nan?

LILY: Tell anyone what?

(*JEM thinks LILY's mind has slipped again. But LILY winks at him.*)

(*Laughs.*) *I got alka-selter!*

(*JEM smiles and passes the spliff back.*)

(*Smiles.*) Ye're a good boy, Jem.

(*Pause.*)

JEM: Stars are startin' ter cum out now.

(*LILY takes the binoculars and looks through them the wrong way.*)

LILY: I like the stars. I like the way they twinkle.

(*JEM reverses them. They laugh.*)

JEM: 'S the atmosphere meks 'em do that. They dun't twinkle really.

LILY: 'Course they twinkle: *Twinkle, twinkle, little star*
    – wouldn't have writ that if they dun't twinkle.

JEM: They on'y *appear* t' twinkle. Beyond the atmosphere…

LILY: *How ah wonder what you are?*

    (*Pause.*)

JEM: The universe is such a big, big place, an' we're on'y a
    tiny part of it; a little speck of blue light – a grain of sand.

LILY: Divn't exaggerate, Jem.

JEM: Ah mean it. There's more stars in universe than there
    are grains of sand on every beach in the whole world.

LILY: *Bullshit!* That en't true. Need a kick up the arse, you.

JEM: Aye… What if there en't no intelligent life out there?
    What if there's no God? What if there's just us an' tha's it?

LILY: Wha's wrong wi' that?

JEM: If this life is all we got an' we mess it up…?

LILY: Yer bloody worry too much, you.

    (*Pause.*)

    Ah'm ever so happy.

JEM: Are yer?

LILY: Ah like it 'ere wi' you an' me herbal relaxation.

JEM: (*Smiles.*) Aye, 's nice, en't it?

LILY: Ah divn't like all that shoutin' tha's bin goin' on, though.

JEM: No, nor me.

LILY: Ah doan't know wha's wrong wi' yer Dad.

JEM: No.

LILY: Ever such a happy lad he were.

JEM: Yeah?

LILY: Used ter tek his clothes off in corn.

JEM: (*Laughs.*) Wouldn't do that now.

LILY: Allus smilin' he were. Wish he'd smile again…ah worry
    about him.

    (*Pause.*)

JEM: It wor better when we wor little; he had more time for
    us then. He liked me more then, I think.

LILY: Ah know what he needs…

JEM *and* LILY: …*a good kick up the arse!* (*Laugh.*)

LILY: Things'll sort 'emselves out.

JEM: Yer reckon?

LILY: You go in a tunnel; you gorra come out where there's light.

JEM: Hope so.

LILY: *'Hope so?'* Bloody pederast, you are.

JEM: *Pessimist,* Nan.

LILY: Tha's what ah said… Aas ever so tired.

JEM: Have yer a little lie down, if yer like.

LILY: Think ah'll have me a lie down.

JEM: Ah'll wake yer when I head back.

LILY: Wake me when ye're headin' back, will yer?

JEM: Aye, I'll wake yer.

LILY: (*Lying down.*) Shame about the cows.

> (*LILY, now in the corn, instantly falls asleep. Pause. JEM swigs a can of beer.*)

JEM: (*Sings.*) *Twinkle, twinkle, little star…* (*Speaks.*) *How ah wonder what you are?*

> (*Something stirs over the boundary fence.*)

> Who's there?! *Cum out if yer wanna mek contact!*

> (*DAVE steps out of the long grass.*)

DAVE: Hiya Jem.

JEM: (*Delighted.*) *Dave!* Oh Dave! Nice one! Oh Dave, mate! Where've yer bin?! I en't half missed yer… Ah mean like a mate misses his mate sort o' thing, not in a sexual way.

DAVE: Glad to hear it.

JEM: Doan't know why I said that.

DAVE: What?

JEM: About the sexual way thing… I mean, 's obvious, en't it?

DAVE: Jem?

JEM: Aye?

DAVE: Shut up an' giz a can –

JEM: *Right on…!* (*Passes a can, delighted again.*) Aw Dave, Dave! It's so good t' see yer, mate… I thought yer wor off ter Cyprus, like.

DAVE: Two weeks' time.

JEM: Oh…'s a shame, en't it? Ah'll miss seein' yer, mate.

DAVE: Ditto, Jem ditto… (*Clank cans in a toast.*) How's Jule?

JEM: Oh… Oh, you doan't wanna know, mate. Bin mopin' round the place like a reet bitch.

DAVE: What d'yer think's causin' that?

JEM: Er… *PMT?*

DAVE: No, I mean do you think it's got anythin' t' do with me?

JEM: Oh reet! Could be, could be – who knows wi' her. I think she's crazy not ter snap you up; I mean ah'm on'y sayin' as a mate.

DAVE: I know that.

JEM: Good.

DAVE: So, she mentioned me at all?

JEM: Er…no, can't say she has.

DAVE: Right.

JEM: But who knows what she thinks. She's not one ter gie much away. But ter tell yer the truth, 's arl bin a bit grim around 'ere.

DAVE: She still upset about the cows?

JEM: Big time, mate, an' the general state o' things… Ah've had a bit of a tough time too.

DAVE: Why? Wha's up, Jem?

JEM: Ah…doan't know if I can tell yer.

DAVE: What?

JEM: Ye're a mate, en't yer?

DAVE: 'Course I am, you know that, Jem.

JEM: Ah mean I feel I can talk ter yer; tell yer things.

DAVE: I'm a mate.

JEM: Secret things.

DAVE: 'S up t'you, Jem.

JEM: I… I think ah wanna be a girl.

DAVE: Yeah?

JEM: Yeah, can't explain it. 'S like ah'm trapped in wrong body.

DAVE: I see.

JEM: Bet yer thinks ah'm a right weirdo?

DAVE: No, no I don't, Jem.

JEM: Ah've got a pair of Jule's panties on reet now.

DAVE: (*Laughs.*) I'm sorry, Jem. But that *is* funny! Does she know?

JEM: Gid 'em me.

DAVE: Which ones?

JEM: Flesh coloured, bits o' lace round bottom.

DAVE: I like those ones. She gave you *those* ones?

JEM: An' some more; got quite a collection.

DAVE: You should look into gettin' a sex change, Jem.

JEM: Ah'd love one.

DAVE: Well go for it.

JEM: (*Excited.*) Oh, ah'd love to!

DAVE: 'S a bit of a shocker, mate. But well, y'know, takes all sorts t' make a world.

JEM: Think ah could get one, get an operation?

DAVE: People do.

JEM: Ah'm ganna look into it.

DAVE: See yer doctor.

JEM: Ah will! Dad wants me too anyroad. That'll show the miserable twat!

DAVE: You'd have to change your name, though.

JEM: I hadn't thought o' that. What d'yer reckon, Dave? What would suit me?

DAVE: Bloody hell, Jem. How should I know?

JEM: Ye're brilliant, Dave! Ye're brilliant!

DAVE: You're not gonna kiss me, are yer?

JEM: *No!*

DAVE: (*Laughs.*) I'm only jokin'!

JEM: (*Smiles.*) Aye.

DAVE: I still don't want you t' kiss me, though.
 (*JULE approaches.*)

JULE: (*Calls.*) *Jem! Nan! Tea's ready!*

JEM: Oh I can't wait t' see her face when she sees you again.

JULE: (*Calls.*) *Jem!*

JEM: (*Calls back.*) *Aye?*

JULE: *Get yer arse in gear, yer lazy tosser!*

JEM: *Jule!*

JULE: (*Getting pissed off.*) *What?!*

JEM: *Cum 'ere!*

JULE: *Piss off! Ah'm busy!*

JEM: *You gorra cum 'ere, Jule!*

JULE: *What is it?*

JEM: *Quick! You gorra come 'ere!*

JULE: (*Rushes on.*) What is it? Is it Nan? She alreet…?

  (*JULE is confronted by DAVE. Pause.*)

  *Dave…?* Thought yer wor in Cyprus.

DAVE: A couple of weeks.

JULE: Oh.

DAVE: Thought I'd jump the fence one last time; see if I could catch you.

JULE: I see.

DAVE: An'… I have.

JULE: Aye…well…

DAVE: So…how…?

JULE: Well, 's arl a bit…

DAVE: Yeah, Jem told me.

JULE: Got a lot ter sort out 'ere now.

DAVE: Sounds serious.

JULE: It is… Why en't yer rung me?

DAVE: Why haven't *you* rung *me?*

JULE: Oh, 's *my* fault is it?

DAVE: I told you I was goin' away. Ball's in your court.

JULE: Typical bloody male reaction.

DAVE: You dumped me, Jule.

JULE: Wha's that got ter do wi' it?

DAVE: So – you bin missin' me?

JULE: *'Missin' yer?'* (*Tearful.*) 'Course I have, you bastard!
  (*She hugs him, crying.*)

DAVE: Oh sweetheart!

JULE: Babe! *Oh babe!*

DAVE: I don't half love you!

JULE: Ah doan't half love *you!*

DAVE: It'll be great in Cyprus. I've checked out the accommodation.

JULE: What?

DAVE: We don't have to stay in army property; we can rent a small villa.

JULE: What yer talkin' about?

DAVE: You an' me in Cyprus.

JULE: Ah'm not goin' ter Cyprus.

DAVE: Well…how are we gonna…? I mean how will I see you?

JULE: Ah dunno…when ye're on leave; an' I can cum ower there now an' again, stay in villa.

JEM: Has it got a swimmin' pool?

DAVE: What?

JEM: I jest wondered if it had a swimmin' pool.

DAVE: I don't know…I think so.

JEM: Be great! Ah could visit an' arl – few cans round pool; be great.

DAVE: Jule, you just said you loved me.

JULE It doan't mean ah'm ganna gie up farmin'.

DAVE: The farm's finished; you know that.

JULE: The farm en't finished, actually; much as ye'd like it ter be. The farm's about to enter a new stage, actually.

DAVE: Be reasonable, for God's sake!

JULE: Cum wanderin' back 'ere wi' yer plans all med; expectin' me ter run after yer like a bloody dog!

DAVE: At least I'm bein' realistic!

JULE: You en't me lord 'n' master!

DAVE: What you talkin' about?

JULE: Snap yer fingers an' ah'll jump!

DAVE: God, now I know why I stayed away!

JULE: Aye?

DAVE: Stubborn moody cow!

JULE: Yer doan't like what yer see – *piss off!*

DAVE: Right – if that's what you want.

JULE: Think I need you in me life? Foller yer t' Cyprus, so's ah'm at yer beck an' call. *No thanks!*

DAVE: I don't know why I bothered!

JULE: Nor me!

DAVE: Sod you!

JULE Up yours!

DAVE: (*Climbing the fence.*) Bollocks!

JULE: You en't got none!

(*DAVE exits. Pause.*)

JEM: Did that just 'appen?

JULE: (*Calls.*) Dave! Dave...!! Oh, what have I done?! This is *your* fault!

JEM: Normally is.

JULE: Oh God! I wanna die!

(*JULE runs off back to the house.*)

JEM: Know how yer feel... Better get back, ah s'pose. C'mon Nan – (*Calls.*) Nan!

(*He goes into the corn to wake her.*)

(*Alarmed.*) *Nan!* Oh no...oh no, please?

(*He pulls her limp body up.*)

Nan – speak ter me? Nan – stars are twinklin' – look. Look – (*Cries.*) Oh Nan...yer can't leave me 'ere...yer can't.

(*Music. Lights fade to blackout.*)

# Scene 3

*The house. The family are dressed in black. The remnants of the funeral wake about the room: sandwiches, bottles of beer, etc. BEN is at the front door, seeing off the last guest. As the front door closes we hear a car pulling away and BEN enters, clearly tanked up.*

BEN: Last on 'em gone. On'y time we see her is when there's a funeral.

MAGS: Everybody's so busy these days.

JULE: Nice flowers.

BEN: Aye, nice flowers. Good send off, ah s'pose.

(*BEN grabs the whisky bottle.*)

MAGS: *Ben* –

BEN: 'S a funeral, Mags. Everybody drinks at funerals.

MAGS: Ye've had a skinful.

BEN: Ah know, Mags, but it's me Mam, like. Ah'm upset, en't I? (*BEN begins to pour the whisky into a glass, but in his drunken state, spills some. JEM shoots him a look.*) What you lookin' at, Kylie?

JULE: *Leave him alone!*

MAGS: Alreet, calm down everybody; we're arl upset.

BEN: Aye…sorry, ah just er…'s the er…

JULE: Booze?

BEN: *The occasion.* 'S me Mam, en't it?

JEM: Ah miss her… Ah doan't half miss her.

MAGS: Allus chasin' after her, I were. Never knew where she'd end up.

JULE: 'Ole chicken shed.

JEM: JCB bucket.

MAGS: (*Laughs.*) Convinced we kept movin' her room.

JEM: 'N' she'd get up at five o'clock in mornin' ter pick flowers.

JULE: (*Affectionately.*) Aye, barmy ole git.

BEN: Weren' allus barmy; good mother she were. Good mother. Good farmer an' arl. She an' Dad ran this place like clockwork. Worked hard, but…ah dunno; had summat ter show fer it then.

JULE: We will again, Dad.

(*BEN suddenly looks uncomfortable. He's come to a decision.*)

BEN: *Jule…* Well all on yer, really – I had ter do it, like.

JULE: Oh God, wha's cummin' now?

BEN: Doan't mek this hard fer me –

MAGS: Wha's goin' on, Ben?

BEN: (*Struggling.*) There's debts, see. Big debts. Had ter sell summat. I had no choice; ye've gorra understand that. I mean ah've really struggled wi' it all. Me 'ead's spinnin', like.

JULE: What have yer done now? You en't sold our tractor, have yer?

MAGS: Mebbe this en't the time fer arl this?

JULE: He brought it up – *wha's he done?* Ah've got a right ter know if it affects me.

BEN: Things've bin bad; worse than bad, actually. I kept it
    from yer. But now, well 's arl got a bit…

JULE: *You sold our tractor?*

BEN: No.

JULE: *Thank God!*

BEN: Our milk-quota.

    (*Pause.*)

JULE: Can yer say that again? Ah doan't think ah can be
    'earin' right. I thought fer a second you said ye'd sold our
    milk-quota.

BEN: Ah'm sorry, Jule.

MAGS: *Milk-quota?!*

BEN: Bank's bin insistin' we pay summat back.

JULE: But Dad, what yer playin' at? We'll get compensation;
    money fer cleanin' up an' arl; use some o' that ter settle debts.

BEN: It en' enough, en't half enough.

MAGS: Yer sold our quota?

BEN: Had to; 's the bank, en't it?

JULE: *Oh Christ!*

MAGS: No, no wait, Jule. It en't arl lost; get straight, plant
    some cash crops an' we can buy it back in a few years.

JULE: The milkin' gear'll've seized up by then.

BEN: I got a buyer for the milkin' gear.

JULE: What?

BEN: One o' them big farms ower at Santon Bridge says
    they'll tek the lot off me hands. Crap price, but it's a
    buyers' market.

    (*Pause.*)

    Ah've bin dreadin' tellin' yer. Ah bin dreadin' it.

JULE: I doan't know what ter say.

BEN: What could ah do? Had no choice.

MAGS: Least yer could do is consult yer family. We all live
    an' work here, yer know.

BEN: 'S *my* responsibility.

JULE: I can't believe ye'd do this!

BEN: Want a roof ower yer 'ead?

MAGS: I know things've bin bad…

BEN: The farm just en't economical anymore; can't mek it work. Ah've tried, by God ah've tried, but aas at me wits' end.

MAGS: Yer shouldn't've kept us in dark. You should've shared this wi' all on us.

JULE: Aye an' mebbe we could've done summat ter save the dairy.

BEN: What could you have done that I couldn't?

JULE: Ah've got ideas, but ye've never listened ter me, never. Ah'm twenty-one years old an' arl ah've ever done is wander round fields up ter me knees in shit. *What fer?!*

BEN: Aye, what fer, eh? (*Swigs bottle.*).

JEM: (*Shouts.*) *Shurrup!!* Just shurrup!! *My Nan's dead…!!* (*Quieter.*) My Nan's dead an' arl you lot can do is nark at each other. We should be rememberin' her, not slaggin' each other off!

MAGS: (*Hugs JEM.*) She's in a better place now, Jem.

JEM: What if there en't a better place? What if this is it? What if this is arl there is?

MAGS: C'mon…s' ganna be alreet.

JEM: Ah miss her.

MAGS: Ah know yer do.

BEN: Aye, c'mon. Let's bury the hatchet, eh? 'Specially terday.

MAGS: Aye, we'll talk about farm another time.

(*BEN, now in a reconciliatory frame of mind, tries to hug JULE. But he's drunk and she simply freezes, disgusted.*)

BEN: Alreet, girl? We alreet?

JULE: Yer stink o' booze.

BEN: (*Hugs her.*) C'mere, stop bein' clever; it divn't suit yer. (*But JULE still doesn't reciprocate.*) Yer Mam's reet – no more worryin' about what might 'appen tomorra'. (*He pats her back.*) Ye're a good girl. Aye, ye're a bloody good 'n'! Aye… (*He releases her.*) An' yer Nan – well she wor one o' best, she were…

(*BEN opens a can of beer.*)

Here son – have a beer, eh?

JEM: (*Takes it.*) Ta.

BEN: Put hairs on yer chest, eh?

JEM: Aye.

BEN: Ye'll be alreet, Jem. Swig it down, lad – it helps.

JULE: Well *you'd* know.

MAGS: Gie it a rest you two.

BEN: Ah'm his Dad, Jule; aas jest showin' some concern.

JULE: Be the first time.

BEN: Hey, hey I know yer think ah've bin foolish…

JULE: *Think?*

BEN: …but I worry about all on yer if yer on'y knew…all on yer. Ye're still my weans. Yer sin the doctor yet, lad?

MAGS: Saw him t'other day. Ah took him. Poor lad's in a reet state.

BEN: (*Surprised.*) Good…good. What did he say then?

JEM: Well…if ye're really interested…?

BEN: 'Course I am, Jem – ye're my lad.

JEM: Okay well…first of all ah'm gerrin' me some psychological counsellin', try an' get me 'ead straight… 'cause yer know, well ah'm in a bit of a mess.

BEN: Ye're doin' the reet thing. He's doin' the reet thing, en't he Mags?

MAGS: Ah think so.

JEM: Then ah can move on ter next stage if ah want.

BEN: Oh aye, wha's the next stage, then?

JEM: Gender assessment programme.

BEN: I told yer it could be sorted.

JEM: 'N' then I could start livin' as a woman if I like.

BEN: Yer what?

JEM: Yer know; dressin' as a woman, livin' that lifestyle.

BEN: How is that s'posed ter cure yer?

JEM: The operation'd do that.

BEN: Operation? What operation? They en't gonna cut a

bit of yer brain off, are they? You en't havin' one o' them
colostomies, lad. They can leave yer stupid, they can.

JEM: It en't me brain they'd be cuttin' off.

BEN: Well, what then?

MAGS: He might want a sex change.

BEN: What?

MAGS: He's thinkin' about changin' his sex.

BEN: But…yer took him t' doctor…why…? Ah doan't get it.

MAGS: If it's what he wants…

BEN: *He can't have it!*

JEM: Please Dad, try an' understand?

BEN: *Understand?* Understand my bloody arse! I en't havin'
no son o' mine growin' tits!

MAGS: Well ye'll just have ter get used to it wun't yer?

BEN: Ah'll be the laughin' stock!

JULE: Allus thinkin' o' yerself.

BEN: *Perverted little swine!*

MAGS: Tha's enough!

BEN: Bet he's wearin' knickers now! Ah bet he is! Wearin'
frilly bloody knickers at his old Nan's funeral! No bloody
respect!

JEM: You shut up!! Ah loved her!

BEN: *Loved her?!* It wor you what killed her!

MAGS: I said that's enough!

JEM: *I never!* Dun't say that!

BEN: Killed her wi' drugs!

JEM: I din't kill her. Say it wern't me?! Ah couldn't live wi' it.
Ah would never've harmed her.

MAGS: You din't kill her, Jem. Her time were up, tha's arl.
An' better now than later when she lost it altogether.

JEM: She said she wor happy – she told me.

BEN: She told you that?

JEM: Before she died, she told me. Said she wor worried
about you an' arl…how yer dun't smile no more.
(*Pause.*)

BEN: I...er...ah divn't know what ah'm sayin', son... I din't mean... I shouldn't've said what ah said.

JULE: No yer shouldn't!

(*Doorbell rings.*)

MAGS: (*Sighs.*) Ah'll get it.

(*MAGS exits.*)

BEN: But you en't havin' no bloody sex change! No way, José!

JEM: Ah divn't care either way. Wha's the point? Wha's the point of anythin'?

(*MAGS enters, followed by DAVE, dressed in civvies, with a carrier-bag.*)

MAGS: It's Dave.

JULE: Oh...oh, hello Dave.

DAVE: Hiya Jule.

BEN: Wha's he doin' 'ere?

DAVE: I've erm...well I've come to pay my respects.

BEN: You got a bloody nerve, en't yer?

MAGS: Oh Ben – shut up, will yer?

BEN: Disease came from somewhere, din't it? 'N' he wor on land *after* restrictions were in place.

MAGS: Stop bein' ridiculous.

BEN: Bloody coincidence though en't it?

MAGS: I said shut up, Ben!

JEM: Hiya Dave.

DAVE: Hi Jem!

BEN: What yer got in yer bag? Chocolates ah'll bet. Chocolates ter charm the women, eh?

DAVE: (*Hands the carrier to BEN.*) I bought you a curry.

BEN: (*Taken aback.*) Oh...well...thanks.

DAVE: *Extra chilles.*

BEN: Could allus eat a curry.

(*BEN begins to open the curry, gets a fork and tucks in.*)

DAVE: Jule said yer like extra chillies. Jule –

JULE: Aye?

DAVE: You okay?

JULE: Not really.

DAVE: Sorry about your Nan.

JULE: Aye thanks… How's things then?

DAVE: Busy. We've been gettin' the unit sorted. We're off on Friday.

JULE: Aye I know.

DAVE: Yeah… 'S difficult this.

JULE: Yeah.

DAVE: It's not the time or place I know, but…

JULE: What Dave?

DAVE: I just wanna say thanks, I s'pose.

JULE: What fer?

DAVE: Everythin'. 'S been great. I'll never forget you.

JULE: Ditto. (*Smiles.*)

BEN: (*Coughs, embarassed.*) Nice! Nice 'n' hot. Got chillies jest right.

DAVE: So –

JULE: So –

DAVE: I'll…erm, I suppose I'd better…

MAGS: Can ah get you a drink, Dave?

DAVE: I don't want to…

MAGS: It's no trouble.

JEM: Have a beer, Dave –

DAVE: Thanks Jem, if you're sure…

MAGS: It's no trouble, honest.

   (*JEM gets him a can.*)

DAVE: (*Opens can.*) Well – here's to Lily, eh…? I mean to her memory, like.

ALL: (*They all toast, appropriately.*) *To Nan… Mam… Lily.*

DAVE: I don't think I'll ever forget her – I've got the scar (*Laughs.*) …I didn't mean anything… (*Suddenly.*) Jule – come with me sweetheart?

JULE: *Oh Dave…!*

DAVE: It's stupid this. We're meant to be you an' me; you know we are.

JULE: Ah dunno Dave, ah…

DAVE: I love you, you love me; you know you do.

BEN: Alreet then, tha's enough –

DAVE: Come on, darlin'; we could have a great future you an' me – I know it.

BEN: Tha's enough, soldier boy.

MAGS: Shut up Ben!

DAVE: Give it a go, darlin'.

BEN: Ah know what he wants, Jule. Wants ter knock yer up he does; pop a few sprogs out o' yer.

DAVE: What are you talkin' about?

BEN: Ah know, matey boy; ah know what you soldiers are like.

DAVE: You know nothin' about me, nothin'. But yeah, maybe I do want Jule to have our children some day. What's wrong with wantin' a family? watchin' kids grow up?

BEN: Ah could tell yer.

DAVE: You've got a great family. You just don't know it.

BEN: Doan't you tell me what my family is…! *Oh, I know what all this is about* – tryin' ter butter me up, eh? Tha's why ye've bought me a curry. Correction – *crap curry!* Chillies?! Tastes more like a bloody Korma! An' the meat's all gristley!

(*He throws the curry in the bin.*)

MAGS: Oh, 'ere we go –

BEN: Defile me daughter, kill me cattle…

DAVE: Think I wanted to do that?

BEN: 'Course yer did – enjoyed it yer did. Get one ower on the local yokels! Yer think ah'm a joke, dun't yer?

DAVE: Well, at the moment…

BEN: Go on – 'ave a laugh at my expense: the sad, pathetic, drunken waster of a farmer.

DAVE: It's not that funny.

BEN: 'N' yer think yer can wander in 'ere an' tek me daughter away?

JULE: Well what is there ter stay fer anyroad? Milk-quota's gone, our dairy gear's bin sold. This en't a farm anymore, it's jest a great big empty house!

BEN: 'S all your fault anyway; riskin' it all fer a quick shag in corn. *You slag!*

DAVE: How can you talk to yer daughter like that?

BEN: Ah'm her father – I can talk to her how ah like.

DAVE: Look, I've got to go, Jule. Because if I stay any longer I might just deck him.

BEN: Oh aye? Think ye're hard enough, eh? (*Squares up.*) Cum on then, cum on, put 'em up –

MAGS: Stop it Ben!

BEN: I can look after meself an' arl. Ah divn't need to hide behind a gun.

DAVE: You're pathetic!

(*DAVE exits.*)

BEN: (*Calls after him.*) Aye, sod off ter bloody Cyprus an' stay there!

(*Pause.*)

That showed him. That showed him, eh? Cummin' 'ere tryin' ter split up my family. Cummin' here wi' his crappy curry *an' no Nan bread, either!*

JULE: What am ah doin'? Ah divn't wanna be 'ere with you arguin' every day, growin' older every day, wonderin' what the future's ganna bring.

BEN: Ahh, cum on – ye're a farmer, Jule – 's in yer blood; dirt under yer fingernails.

JULE: Ah've got dirt all ower me. Ye've no idea what ah've given up fer this place…what ah've sacrificed.

BEN: *Sacrifice?* What d'you know about that? What have you ever sacrificed that I en't three times over?

JULE: My baby.

BEN: What?

JULE: Ah've had an abortion.

BEN: What…? When…?

MAGS: Couple o' weeks ago.

JEM: Ah wondered where ye'd gone.

JULE: Clinic in Birmingham.

BEN: Well…why'd yer do that?

JULE: Fer you, yer fuckin' idiot. Fer you an' this place.

BEN: Now doan't yer go blamin' me fer summat like that, lass…

JULE: Why not? Thought you wor inter responsibilty?

BEN: Tha's nowt ter do wi' me, that.

JULE: Well would you have bin happy wi' a little bastard runnin' about place? A *soldier's* little bastard?!

BEN: Nowt ter do wi' me.

JULE: What would yer mates've said up the pub, eh?

BEN: You med that decision, lass.

JULE: No Dad, you wor there reet behind it. Ah wor allus tryin' ter live up ter your expectations; allus tryin' ter be the farmer yer wanted me ter be... Now what do I do? (*Cries.*) Now what do I do? I lost everythin'...

JEM: He can't have gone far, Jule.

JULE: No?

JEM: Half way cross meadow by now, ah reckon.

JULE: What d'yer think, Jem?

JEM: Ah think he'll understand. Ah do honestly, Jule. He loves yer, an' ye're not dirty, ye're not bad; really ye're not.

JULE: What d'yer think, Mam?

MAGS: 'S worth a try en't it?

JULE: Alreet –

(*JULE begins to exit.*)

BEN: Desertin' the sinkin' ship, are yer?

JULE: No – jest you.

BEN: Doan't go, Jule... I...ah'm sorry if I...

JULE: You don't want me around, Dad. Ah'm jest an embarrassment. Ah'm a slag, en't I?

(*Just as she's leaving.*)

MAGS: Jule...good luck.

JULE: Well whatever 'appens I en't cummin' back 'ere again.

BEN: Aye, go on – piss off ter soldier boy, see if I care!

(*JULE exits with tears in her eyes.*)

JEM: Where am I ganna go, what am I ganna do?

BEN: Join the circus – they like freaks.

JEM: Good idea. Thanks Dad.

(*JEM exits.*)

BEN: Why did ah say that?

MAGS: Why d'you say half the things yer say? Ah doan't know you anymore. You en't the man ah married. He wor kind, had a sense o' humour, cared fer his family.

(*MAGS begins to exit.*)

BEN: Where yer gannin' now?

MAGS: Clear up yer mess again. See if Jem's alreet.

BEN: What about me? I en' alreet.

MAGS: So do summat about it. *Alcoholic!*

(*MAGS exits.*)

BEN: Extra chilles my arse! More like a bloody Korma...! What a mess! What a bloody mess! Ah'm ridiculous! Ah'm like a bloody...*ridiculous person!* (*Tearful.*) Oh Mam! Me old Mam! *Yer daft ol' sod.* At least you din't 'ave ter face reality to the bitter end: fate spared yer that fate. *'Fate spared yer that fate?'* Wha's that s'posed ter mean? I even *talk* like a twat! (*Pause.*)

What am ah ganna do?

(*Pause. He swigs whisky and then looks over to his gun. Eventually he gets up, takes shells from the drawer, sits at the table and swigs at the bottle again. He purposely breaks the gun and inserts the shells. Another swig of whisky. He puts the barrel in his mouth and closes his eyes, but he hears someone coming and quickly puts the gun down. MAGS enters. She goes to the stove to make coffee.*)

Jem alreet?

MAGS: He's lyin' down. Ganna mek him a hot drink.

BEN: (*Nods.*) Should do the trick.

(*MAGS suddenly notices the gun.*)

MAGS: What yer doin' wi' yon gun?

BEN: I... I wor ganna clean it.

MAGS: *Now?* Why now?

BEN: Why not?

MAGS: You...you weren't...?

(*BEN looks away from her.*)

You...you wor gun'ter...

BEN: No, I were jest ganna clean it.

MAGS: So it en't loaded, then?

BEN: No, it en't loaded.

(*MAGS picks the gun up.*)

What yer doin'?

(*She holds the barrel to her chest.*)

*No! No Mags, dun't!!*

MAGS: Thought yer said it weren't loaded?

BEN: It is! It *is* loaded! Put it down –

MAGS: No, I dun't think ah will.

BEN: Mags, what yer playin' at?

MAGS: Same as you.

BEN: Please Mags, doan't do 'owt daft!

MAGS: Why not? You wor goin' to.

BEN: Please Mags, ah couldn't bear it!

MAGS: An' ah could?

BEN: Aas sorry.

MAGS: Why shouldn't I tek the easy way out? Aas bleedin' inside watchin' me son torture hisself an' me daughter sacrifice everythin' fer a wasted dream.

BEN: Dun't do it, Mags. Ah'm beggin' yer.

MAGS: See what it feels like? Shoe's on t'other foot now, en't it? It en't very nice is it, Ben; watchin' someone yer love destroy themself.

BEN: No…it en't.

MAGS: Think the world revolves around yer, you do. Aas sick o' seein' yer play the martyr, soakin' yer brain in alcohol, feelin' sorry fer yerself all the time…

BEN: Ah'm sorry… I mean ah'm *not* sorry, I'm… I mean ah'll stop feelin' sorry… *Dun't do it, Mags!!*

MAGS: Ah think ah've got to… What is there ter get up fer in mornin' now, eh?

BEN: Well…

MAGS: Stuck fer words, are yer?

BEN: No… I…

MAGS: Ah wanna die…ah *wanna* die.

BEN: Please…think o' the kids?

MAGS: Why? You never have.

BEN: Aas sorry…ah've bin daft.

MAGS: Ah've had all ah can tek round 'ere.

BEN: Dun't pull the trigger – the world'll end if yer do.
>    (*Pause. MAGS slowly places the gun on the table, a little stunned.
>    BEN immediately breaks the gun and removes the shells.*)

MAGS: See what yer nearly med me do.

BEN: (*Tearful.*) D'yer still love me?

MAGS: (*Tearful.*) Aye, 'course I love yer. I love yer more than
>    ah can say.
>    (*MAGS lays into him, pumelling him with her fists.*)
>    So why are yer doin' things like that, you…*bastard?!* What
>    about *me?!*

BEN: Aas sorry.

MAGS: (*Still thumping.*) How d'yer think I feel?

BEN: Aas sorry.

MAGS: (*Still thumping.*) Think ah want ter find yer in, kitchen
>    wi' yer 'ead blown off?!

BEN: No.

MAGS: (*Still thumping.*) What d'yer think that would do ter
>    yer family, you selfish, selfish man!!

BEN: I know… But stop hittin' me now, Mags. Ye're 'urtin' me.
>    (*She stops. They embrace.*)

MAGS: Doan't you ever do that again. Promise me ye'll never
>    do that again?!

BEN: Ah promise. You too, eh?

MAGS: Aye…
>    (*Pause.*)

BEN: *What have I done?*

MAGS: Well ye've gorra face up to it alreet. Tha's what *real*
>    responsibility is all about.

BEN: *I've lost the farm!*

MAGS: Well mebbe you 'ave. But life goes on.

BEN: How can ah move forward now? Ah doan't know know
>    what ter do, Mags.

MAGS: Sometime yer just have ter give up.

BEN: I can't give up!

MAGS: Wha's so wrong wi' admittin' defeat? Why fight ter last drop o' blood? We can't win every battle in life.

BEN: Farm's bin in my family fer generations.

MAGS: It doan't mean ye're obliged ter keep it.

BEN: I put everythin' inter this land; my blood's in soil, 'n' you expect me ter give up? How d'yer think that meks *me* feel?

MAGS: How d'yer think *I* feel? 'S allus me cummin' between everyone; my nerves are worn ter shreds! Ah'm torn apart inside, I am. When does anybody ever put their arms around me an' ask me how I feel?! (*Cries.*)

(*BEN puts his arms around her.*)

BEN: (*Tearful.*) How d'yer feel?

MAGS: *Terrible!*

BEN: Oh…ah'm sorry…aas so sorry…ah've bin ever so selfish, en't I?

MAGS: Ye're 'avin' a breakdown, Ben. Ye've bin 'avin' a breakdown fer past two year.

BEN: Oh! Is that what it is?

MAGS: *'Is that what it is?'* What am ah ganna do wi' you?

BEN: Ah'll…get me to a doctor, eh?

MAGS: Be a start.

BEN: Cut down on booze.

MAGS: Now ye're talkin'. We can salvage summat, still. Dave is a nice lad. 'N' if they can sort things out t'gether, then we're lucky our little girl has met someone she wants ter spend her life with. But you have said some terrible things to her.

BEN: Aye.

MAGS: 'N' ye'd better apologise ter Jem an' arl.

BEN: Aye, ah'll mek it up to him somehow. Ah'll buy him a present…some scent, eh?

MAGS: Well…mebbe. But it en't presents he needs – it's a Dad.

BEN: Does he really want ter be a girl?

MAGS: I dun't think he knows what he wants. But if that's

what he decides then we've gorra support him – he's still our child.

BEN: Melvin Breslaw's lass is a lesbian. Serves in Crown sometimes.

MAGS: 'N' people doan't mek a fuss, do they?

BEN: No...they doan't. I en't havin' *him* behind bar, though... I mean, yer know – wearin' a dress 'n' that; havin' me mates chattin' him up like he's a lass.

MAGS: (*Sighs.*) Let's go an' talk to 'em, eh?

BEN: Aye...ah'll jest have me one last drink.

MAGS: You tek another swig an' ah'm off an' arl.

(*Pause.*)

BEN: Yer mean it, doan't yer?

MAGS: Definitely.

BEN: If ah lost you that'd be the end.

MAGS: There's on'y so much ah can tek.

(*BEN pours the whisky down the sink.*)

BEN: Close shave, eh?

MAGS: Very close... C'mon –

BEN: (*Exiting.*) Tell yer one thing –

MAGS: Aye?

BEN: I shouldn't've chucked that curry away – chillies wor spot on.

MAGS: (*Smiles.*) C'mon –

(*They begin to exit.*)

BEN: You swore.

MAGS: I never!

BEN: You did – you said *bastard*.

MAGS: Divn't use language like that; I keep tellin' yer.

BEN: But yer did Mags, when yer lost it like, yer said...

MAGS: Ah'm warnin' you –

BEN: But yer did.

MAGS: *Did I?*

BEN: Mebbe not.

(*They exit. Music. Lights fade to blackout.*)

# Epilogue

*Twelve months later. BEN is alone in the cornfield. It's a cold night and the stars are twinkling. BEN is looking at the night sky, something he hasn't done for a long time. He is totally absorbed. MAGS enters and joins him.*

MAGS: 'S a lovely night.

BEN: Cold.

MAGS: First frost o' the year, ah reckon.

BEN: Could be.

> (*Pause.*)

> *Look at that lot –*

MAGS: Aye, 's a beautiful night, alreet.

BEN: Ah can see why Jem liked it up 'ere so much…see what he wor gerrin' at now…ah mean, when yer stand 'ere an' look up – *well.*

MAGS: It meks yer feel small.

BEN: Puts things into perspective… Wonder if he'll miss it?

MAGS: He's enjoyin' hisself in Cyprus – he's happy.

BEN: Workin' behind a bar?

MAGS: Very popular wi' locals, Jule says.

BEN: Aye?

MAGS: Said so in her last letter. He's doin' all the organisin'; discos an' stuff.

BEN: Least he en't had his nob off.

MAGS: Yet.

BEN: 'S a phase he wor goin' through I reckon.

MAGS: Probably.

> (*Pause.*)

BEN: Ah miss him…miss 'em both.

MAGS: Well we'll see 'em this summer.

BEN: First holiday for six year.

MAGS: Be first time out the country fer me. Baby'll be 'ere by then.

BEN: Bloody 'ell – ah'll be a grandfather!

MAGS: (*Laughs.*) Couple of old gits.

BEN: Speak fer yerself.

(*Pause.*)

Should've bin a grandfather *before* now, rightly.

MAGS: Well…no point thinkin' about that.

BEN: Ah do though.

MAGS: 'S one o' them things.

BEN Ah just wonder what it would've bin like, yer know. Ah mean, ah can't help thinkin'… Shouldn't've happened.

MAGS: No, but it did. An' there's nowt we can do about it. We're human an' humans are born ter mek mistakes.

BEN: A baby's like a seed, en't it?

MAGS: What yer gerrin' at?

BEN: Well it is. It's a seed growin' in dark, waitin' fer a chance ter grow an' flourish…some mek it an' some…

(*Pause.*)

It's a big responsibility bein' a farmer… All them seeds ter look after, all them animals ter feed, all that land ter care fer.

MAGS: It's a big responsibility alreet.

BEN: Shouldn't build on it; tha's what I object to. 'S productive land, that is; grow anythin' in that soil. 'S a crime ter build on that. Once it's gone, it's gone ferever. *Executive houses wi' outstandin' views!* Can't afford 'em ourselves – 's bloody criminal!

MAGS: Well it's out of our hands now. Nowt we can do about it.

(*Pause.*)

BEN: How yer doin' wi' packin'?

MAGS: Nearly finished. Lot of it we can leave in barn; collect it later.

BEN: Gorra hand keys ower on Friday, mind.

MAGS: Aye.

(*Pause.*)

BEN: Never thought *ah'd* every be packin' tea chests.

MAGS: No… Still, least we got summat out on it, an' it's a cul-de-sac; lucky ter get a cul-de-sac these days.

BEN: Got me eyes on a bit o' land an' arl.

MAGS: *Ye've gorra be jokin'!*

BEN: Jest a small-holdin' like, yer know. Enough ter scratch a bit of a livin', like.

MAGS: Ben...*let it go.*

BEN: Aye...aye, ye're reet.

(*Pause.*)

Jule ever ask about me?

MAGS: Sometimes...should speak to her next time she phones.

BEN: Aye...ah will.

(*Pause. They both look up at the night sky.*)

This is where Mam died.

MAGS: An' Jule an' Dave med love.

BEN: An' ah ran around when I wor a nipper.

MAGS: Wi'out any clothes on.

BEN: (*Laughs.*) Bit cold fer that now.

MAGS: Oh...ah doan't know.

(*They kiss.*)

BEN: God, 's bin a long time, en't it?

MAGS: Too long.

BEN: Think I've forgotten everythin'.

MAGS: It'll all come back.

(*They begin to walk towards the house. BEN pulls them up.*)

BEN: Ah do love you yer know.

MAGS: Ah know.

BEN: Mags...

MAGS: Aye?

BEN: Ah'm scared...ah've never left home before.

(*They embrace, clinging to each other. Music.*
*Lights fade to blackout.*)

*The End.*

www.ingramcontent.com/pod-product-compliance
Ingram Content Group UK Ltd.
Pitfield, Milton Keynes, MK11 3LW, UK
UKHW031252020325
455690UK00007B/82